THE REFRACTIVE THINKER®

AN ANTHOLOGY OF DOCTORAL WRITERS

VOLUME XV
Nonprofits
Strategies for Effective Management

10th Anniversary Edition

Edited by Dr. Cheryl A. Lentz

THE REFRACTIVE THINKER® PRESS

The Refractive Thinker®: An Anthology of Higher Learning
Vol. XV: Nonprofits: Strategies for Effective Management

The Refractive Thinker® Press
www.RefractiveThinker.com
blog: www.DissertationPublishing.com

 Please visit us on Facebook and like our Fan page.
www.facebook.com/refractivethinker

All rights reserved. No part of this book may be reproduced or transmitted in any form or by any means, graphic, electronic or mechanical, including photocopying, recording, taping, Web distribution, or by any informational storage and retrieval system without written permission from the publisher except for the inclusion of brief quotations in a review or scholarly reference.

Books are available through The Refractive Thinker® Press at special discounts for bulk purchases for the purpose of sales promotion, seminar attendance, or educational purposes. Special volumes can be created for specific purposes and to organizational specifications. Please contact us for further details.

Individual authors own the copyright to their individual materials.
The Refractive Thinker® Press has each author's permission to reprint.

Copyright © 2018 by The Refractive Thinker® Press
Managing Editor: Dr. Cheryl A. Lentz • DrCherylLentz@gmail.com

Library of Congress Control Number: 2013945437

BUSINESS & ECONOMICS / Nonprofit Organizations & Charities / Management & Leadership

ISBN: 978-1-7329382-0-5
*Kindle and electronic versions available

Refractive Thinker® logo by Joey Root; The Refractive Thinker® Press logo design by Jacqueline Teng; cover design and production by Gary A. Rosenberg.

Printed in the United States of America

10   9   8   7   6   5   4   3   2   1

Contents

Testimonials v

Foreword ix

Preface xiii

Acknowledgments xv

CHAPTER 1
Dr. Natalie Casale 1
Like Us, Follow Us, Support Us

CHAPTER 2
Dr. Julee H. Hafner 21
What Nonprofit Organizations Need to Unlearn

CHAPTER 3
Dr. Frank Musmar 45
Financial Distress at Nonprofit Organizations

CHAPTER 4
Dr. Avideh Sadaghiani-Tabrizi & Dr. Teresa Lao 69
Managing Nonprofit Inevitable Cyber-Vulnerabilities

CHAPTER 5
Dr. Barbara J. Yancy-Tooks 87
A Critical Perspective on Selection Practices in Texas Community Colleges

CHAPTER 6
Dr. Denise J. La Salle & Dr. Alexandro Beato 105
Strategies to Reduce Employee Turnover in Higher Education

CHAPTER 7
Dr. Evelyn Hollis 131
Development: A Praxis for Constructive Management and Dynamic Leadership

CHAPTER 8
Dr. Toscha L. Dickerson 147
Methods to Reducing the Rate of Recidivism Among Women

CHAPTER 9
Dr. Samuel Hayes, Jr. 163
Nonprofit: U.S. Leaders' Experiences With Developing Global Networks

CHAPTER 10
Dr. Julie Ducharme, Dr. Karen Walker & Dr. Cheryl Lentz 187
Non-profit Transition Strategies: Combat Boots to Heels Program

Index 205

2018 Catalog 207

Testimonials

Greg Reid
CEO/Founder of Secret Knock
http://www.secretknock.co/
Many often quit 5 minutes before the miracle happens. Dr. Cheryl Lentz and the Refractive Thinker® series' contributing scholars value the importance of seeking answers to business problems within their research to serve others with what they've learned. This powerful book shares powerful contributions for those in the business of serving others in the world of nonprofits. Lean in, learn, read, and apply this cutting-edge information so that you don't quit 5 minutes before the miracle happens. Remember, to get what you want, you have to serve others to help them get what they want first.

Clarissa Burt
CEO/Founder of *The EnvelopHer.com* Movement
https://clarissaburt.com/
Learning doesn't always happen in a formal classroom; sometimes one learns from the school of hard knocks and experience, often in serving others. The Refractive Thinker® series looks to connecting these two worlds of business and learning. A refractive thinker® is one who never settles for anything less than everything, daring to dream a bit with a model to change the world of academic publishing by understanding the value of education and research—whatever its source. No

one benefits from playing small, particularly with one's personal passion in the world of nonprofits. Refractive thinkers play on a big stage, truly desiring to change their world and ours. Join them.

Brian Jud

Executive Director of the Association of Publishers for Special Sales, author of 14 books including *How to Make Real Money Selling Books*
http://www.bookmarketingworks.com/

Authors always want to know the latest out-of-the-box strategy to sell more of their books. *The Refractive Thinker®* series adopts this innovative-thinking approach, so you can get your doctoral research out of academia and into the hands of those who need it. This volume, regarding the field of nonprofits, is a particularly good example of how to make that happen. There is no need to go it alone. Join your colleagues on a journey in search of creative and unique solutions as you navigate the landscape of business.

Martha Hanlon

CEO and Founder of Wide Awake Business
https://www.wideawakebusiness.com

Nonprofits seem to be forgotten in our economic push for more, more, more profits. Most management books offer insights for profit-driven companies, but who's offering not-for-profit management proven strategies to improve their leadership? *The Refractive Thinker®* addresses this hole in our vision and knowledge through its latest publication, *Vol XV: Nonprofits: Strategies for Effective Management*. Whether you run or manage a nonprofit or profit-driven company, you'll uncover insights you should apply to your business. The anthology approach insures different perspectives and approaches to open your mind to the possible.

Dr. Kristina Harris

https://www.linkedin.com/in/kristinaharris/
Too many times, nonprofits are started to meet a need or make a difference. The founders are driven by passion and neglect the business strategy. *The Refractive Thinker®: Vol. XV: Nonprofits: Strategies for Effective Management* provides guidance and calls attention to many areas nonprofits neglect. Nonprofits must be visible and competitive. The contributing scholars address areas of weakness and provide strategies for success.

Olvia Parr-Rud, MS

Data Scientist, Bestselling and Award-winning author, and Corporate Love Ambassador
https://www.LoveMakeItYourBusiness.com.
To thrive in today's fast-paced, high-tech, global economy, companies must become more adaptable and resilient. Nonprofits are especially challenged due to their unique structures and financial constraints. *The Refractive Thinker®* series offers powerful, practical insights and strategies for navigating our increasing complex business landscape. The blend of academic rigor with real world applications through the lens of refractive thinking strategies provides unique, cutting-edge solutions. *The Refractive Thinker®: Vol XV: Nonprofits: Strategies for Effective Management* is a potent addition to this series. Every business should make this entire series a staple in their corporate library.

"It always seems impossible until it's done."

"After climbing a great hill, one only finds that there are many more hills to climb."
—Nelson Mandela

FOREWORD
The Power of a Wish

Many people struggle to find their place in the world. For me, finding that purpose was in the eyes of a 7 year old little boy named Chris with leukemia. Meeting this little boy forever changed me and those around me. As one of the primary officers from the Arizona Highway Patrol, we decided to grant Chris's wish to be a Highway Patrol Motorcycle Officer like his heroes, Ponch and John from the television show, "CHiPs." Chris was made the first and only Honorary Arizona Highway Patrol Officer in the history of the Arizona Highway Patrol, complete with a custom made uniform, badge, and Motor Officer Wings. Chris succumbed to his illness a few day after receiving his "wish", and was buried with full police honors in Illinois, as I led the police funeral procession. Because of the power of this wish by one very special little boy, Chris became the inspiration to start a nonprofit foundation that would let other children 'make a wish' and have it come true for them as well.

Never under estimate the power of one; the power of passion, the power to simply take the first step forward and to ask, *what if?* The power of *what if* is one of the tenets of refractive thinking supported by Dr. Cheryl Lentz and her award winning series for doctoral scholars, the Refractive Thinker®. The goal of this series is to embrace this beyond the box thinking of the power of one, the power of having a dream and sharing it with others.

The scholars of this particular volume of *The Refractive Thinker®* is about the passion and perseverance of finding a need to support a cause. Many people often find solving such a need to be a daunting challenge and often lack the courage to take the first step. My answer to them is to find strength in the eyes of our 7 year old little boy Chris who became our hero. While fighting the ultimate battle for his life, Chris inspired us to help him and eventually others like him. The love of a community drew people together powerfully to bring happiness to the last few days of his life, bringing comfort to his family of a community that wanted to make a difference.

We simply asked the question, if we could bring a community together to grant Chris his dying wish and bring happiness and peace to him and his family in his final days, might we grant wishes for other children as they persevere in their life struggles as well? The power of a wish started a movement that was heard around the world . . .

For the scholars of this Nonprofit volume in this *Refractive Thinker*® series, their missions are many, from helping nonprofits unlearn previous knowledge that no longer serves, to overcoming financial distress, selection hiring perspectives, serving the needs of higher education and our veterans, the needs are many, the resources few. The thread that links them is that they believe they can make a difference.

And a child shall lead us is a powerful force where one can find inspiration in our personal lives and communities. Let me encourage you to find your inspiration, to find your purpose in making the world a better place. Have the courage to simply begin, and I assure you that others will follow, as many have in following our worldwide mission for the Make A Wish Foundation. Remember the power of a wish can change the world.

Sincerely,
Frank Shankwitz
The Creator and a Founder of the Make-A-Wish Foundation

About the Author...

Frank Shankwitz is best known as the creator and a founder of the Make-A-Wish Foundation, an extraordinary charity that grants the wishes to children with life-threatening illnesses. From humble beginnings, the Make-A-Wish Foundation is now a global organization that grants a child's wish somewhere in the world on an average of every 28 minutes. Frank is a U.S. Air Force veteran and has a long and distinguished career in law enforcement. He began as a Arizona Highway Patrol Motorcycle Officer and retired as a Homicide Detective with the Arizona Department of Public Safety, with 42 years of service.

Frank has been featured in numerous publications and television programs, and has received several awards, including the White House Call to Service Award from President George W. Bush, and the "Making a Difference In the World" award from the U.S. Military Academy at West Point. In 2015 Frank joined six U.S. Presidents, as well as Nobel Prize winners and industry leaders as a recipient of the Ellis Island Medal of Honor. In December 2015, Frank was presented with an Honorary Doctorate Degree, Doctor of Public Service, from The Ohio State University. In December 2015, Frank was identified as one of the "10 Most Amazing Arizonans" in a front page article in the Arizona Republic newspaper. In January 2016, Frank was identified in a *Forbes Magazine* article as a "Forbes Top Ten Keynote Speaker." In April 2017, Frank was presented the Unite4:Humanity Celebrity ICON Social Impact Award. Frank's new book, *Wishman,* was released in October 2016 and is available at Amazon.com. Frank's life story will soon be featured in an upcoming motion picture, *Wish Man,* which is in pre-production. Further information is available on Frank's **website: wishman1.com**

Preface

Welcome to the award winning **Refractive Thinker® Doctoral Anthology Series**. We are thrilled to have you join us for the 17th Volume in the series (Vol II was published 3 times), *The Refractive Thinker®: Vol. XV: Nonprofits: Strategies for Effective Management*. Join us as we continue to celebrate the accomplishments of doctoral scholars from around the globe.

Our mission continues to be to get research off the coffee table, out of the Ivory Tower of academia, and into the hands of people who cannot only use but benefit from the many insights and wisdom found from doctoral research results. The goal is to continue to bridge the gap from the halls of academia into the halls of the business world. *The Refractive Thinker®* series continues to offer a resource from the many contributing doctoral scholars as they offer their chapter summaries of doctoral research well beyond the boundaries of a traditional textbook. Instead, the goal for this series is to use refractive thinking strategies to push the boundaries beyond conventional wisdom and to explore the paths not yet traveled particularly in this evolving digital age of effective management for nonprofit organizations.

As we approach Fall 2018, this peer-reviewed publication offers readers insights and solutions to various challenges in nonprofit organizations regarding effective management strategies and what nonprofit leaders and managers need to know to achieve success. Our hope is for you to find answers regarding the unique challenges that nonprofits face to help guide your efforts in the boardroom, as well as the work space with both employees and volunteers in particular as part of this special edition *The Refractive Thinker®: Vol XV: Nonprofits: Strategies for Effective Management* that have come from the research and pens of professional academicians and scholars around the world. The premise is to think not only *outside the box*, but also *beyond the box*, to create new solutions, to ask new questions, to proceed forward on new roads not yet explored or traveled. Our premise is to review academic research in a simple to digest executive summary format to offer new ways for business leaders to think about effective practices for strategies in their business based on what new research has to offer specifically growing the future of business.

With this volume, we continue to include a section to the series where Dr. Cheryl Lentz, *The Academic Entrepreneur* concludes each chapter from a business point of view to link this doctoral research to applications for your business.

Remember, not only does *The Refractive Thinker®* series offer a physical book, we offer eBooks (Kindle, Nook, and Adobe eReader), and eChapters (individual chapters by author) that highlight the writings of your favorite Refractive Thinker® scholars, available through our website: http://www.RefractiveThinker.com, as well as www.Amazon.com . Be sure to also visit our social media to include our Facebook page, Twitter, our YouTube Channel, and our groups on LinkedIN® for further discussions regarding the many ideas presented here.

We look forward to your continued support and interest of the more than 150 scholars within *the Refractive Thinker®* doctoral community who contributed to this multi award winning anthology series from around the globe. Our mission that began with Volume 1 many years ago is to bring research out of academia for application in the world of business to provide answers to the many questions asked.

Acknowledgments

The foundation of scholarly research embraces the art of asking questions—to validate and affirm, what we do, and why. Through asking the right questions, the right answers are found. Leaders often challenge the status quo, to offer alternatives and new directions, to dare to try something bold and audacious, to try something that has never been tried before. This 17th publication of our beloved 16-time award winning *Refractive Thinker*® series required the continued belief in this new publishing model, of a peer-reviewed doctoral anthology, by those willing to continue forward on this voyage.

We are grateful for the help of many who made this collaboration possible. First, let me offer a special thank you to our **Peer Review Board**, to include Dr. Karin Mae, Dr. Ron Jones, and myself; and our **Board of Advisors** to include: Brian Jud and Dr. Jody Sandwisch; and media consultant / partner, Rebecca Hall-Gruyter.

My gratitude extends with a well-deserved thank you to our production team: Gary Rosenberg (production specialist) and Joey Root, designer of the original Refractive Thinker® logo.

Thank you. We appreciate everyone's contributions to this scholarly collaboration.

Job well done!
My best to our continued success!

Dr. Cheryl Lentz
Managing Editor and Chief Refractive Thinker®

CHAPTER 1

Like Us, Follow Us, Support Us

Dr. Natalie Casale

A person will create a nonprofit organization (NPO) by establishing a location within the community that provides services of a missing need, such as food, shelter, or education (National Council of Nonprofits, 2018). A fundraising campaign is an important activity for nonprofit organizational leaders to generate donations to support these needs (Jones & Daniel, 2018). Campaigning can be done by mail, email, and social media (Casale, 2015). A social media presence is an inexpensive marketing tactic for these leaders of NPOs to reach out to current donors and attract new donors (Vinerean, 2017). The refractive thinker will investigate the different social media applications, determined to understand the benefits of each, and select one or more that will develop, enhance, or improve the marketing strategies, creating an awareness of the services and needs for donations of the NPO.

Most nonprofit organizational leaders do not invest time or try to develop a social media presence (Nonprofit Tech for Good, 2018). According to Nonprofit Tech for Good (2018), 66,189 of 97,337 (68%) of global non-government organizations do not have a documented social media strategy. According to Feng, Du, and Ling (2017), nonprofit leaders who develop a marketing strategy using social media create an opportunity for promoting engagement and trust and demonstrating activism in the community. Therefore, developing a social media strategy should be a top activity of the NPO leader and will be the focus of this chapter.

A plethora of social media applications exists for NPO leaders to use. Most commonly used are YouTube, Facebook, Twitter, Pinterest, and blogging (Statista, 2018). Creating an account is simple; however, the account must be active to reach out to existing and potential donors about the organization's mission, purpose, needs to inspire, and support the cause (Feng et al., 2017).

The focus of this chapter is to identify strategies an NPO leader can use to develop a social media strategy. The specific problem is NPO leaders do not have social media strategies in writing; therefore, they do not take advantage of reaching out to existing or potential donors with free marketing tools. Generating donations is not an easy task for the NPO leader (Jones & Daniel, 2018); however, understanding the different social media applications and the benefits of each application can fulfill the purpose of the NPO, providing a service to the community in need.

A nonprofit could be local, domestic, and global. Marketing in the NPO could be nonexistent or managed by the founder / CEO, a marketing manager, or a marketing team. In this chapter, the term marketing manager identifies the person in charge of the marketing strategies for the NPO.

Social Media Strategy

According to the Nonprofit Tech for Good (2018), 1,103 of 4,084 (27%) surveyed donors confirmed social media inspires them to support an NPO with donations. For the majority of NPOs without a social media strategy (Public Interest Registry, 2018), this conflict of needs and wants is a missed opportunity of generating donations and awareness of the NPO. Understanding the different benefits of each social media platform will give the NPO leader the opportunity to decide what application meets its organizational needs for generating an awareness of community service offered by the NPO and necessity for donations.

Casale (2015) confirmed Millennials and Generation X prefer advertising of adoptable cats and dogs residing in nonprofit animal rescue organizations of Monmouth County, New Jersey on social media applications Facebook, Twitter, Pinterest, blogging, and Instagram. At the end of 2015, Millennials and Generation X made up the majority of the workforce in the United States (Pew Research Center, 2018), and therefore, is the appropriate groups of people for seeking donations. Each application identified desirable by Millennials and Generation X has its benefits (Casale, 2015); therefore, the marketing manager of the NPO must understand how each social media platform can help create a written social media strategy.

The marketing manager needs to understand the people and community the NPO serves to ensure social media messages and images foster a sense of community (Feng et al., 2017). The messages need to be relevant and images should be in high resolution to ensure followers understand and find the value of these messages (Tafesse & Wien, 2018). Using social media as a marketing medium can be a very powerful tool for the NPO. Anyone with a phone and / or mobile device has access to social media applications that can send messages in a domestic or global audience (Kim & Yu, 2016).

Facebook

Individuals use Facebook to connect to others and like pages that present information in which the individual is interested in, such as companies, brands, celebrities, and causes (Pelletier & Horky, 2015). Businesses use Facebook to create a Facebook page for individuals to like and share information about the business (Musonera & Weber, 2018). These pages present an opportunity for the business to connect to an audience of people interested in the products or services, build brand loyalty, demonstrate the use of products or services, create event pages, and build interests with other potential customers by current fans sharing information presented on page (Pelletier & Horky, 2015). Fans of the page can share their comments of products or services with text, visuals, or videos (Musonera & Weber, 2018).

The NPO marketing manager can use Facebook to create a page for free and can share information about the services of the NPO, such as providing text and visual messages of the NPO's mission, vision, purpose, activities, events, and success stories (Agozzino & Fleck, 2016). The administrator of the NPO's Facebook page can create an event page for fundraisers (Agozzino & Fleck, 2016). Current followers can confirm attendance to an event and share the event with potential donors (Agozzino & Fleck, 2016). Reaching out to others can create additional followers, rallying more people who want to help the cause of the NPO (Agozzino & Fleck, 2016).

The Amyotrophic Lateral Sclerosis (ALS) Association was most successful with a Facebook campaign known as *the ALS Ice Bucket Challenge* (The ALS Association, 2018). This challenge started July 14, 2014, by Chris Kennedy who challenged his cousin to allow him to video a bucket of ice dumped over her head to put a smile on the face of her husband who has ALS (The ALS Association, 2018). This video on his Facebook page inspired a friend to do the same (The ALS Association, 2018). The ALS organization noticed a spike in donations and the inspiration of these donations was from the shared video challenges on Facebook (The ALS Association, 2018). The NPO began a marketing campaign on its Facebook page, sharing the Facebook videos of Kennedy and friends, on August 12, 2014 (The ALS Association, 2018). The campaign went global and included celebrity participants, providing a visual cause and need for the original purpose of the NPO: to raise awareness of the disease, raise money for research, and to provide for the needs for the individuals and their families with the disease (The ALS Association, 2018). The NPO raised $115 million dollars with this campaign (The ALS Association, 2018). The simple sharing of videos of Facebook demonstrated that the NPO marketing managers can use Facebook to share messages about a cause in need and worthy of donations.

Twitter

The main purpose to create and use a Twitter account is to provide text information (Twitter, 2018). A picture or video can be attached to the message; however, users continue to look for current information (Twitter, 2018). Twitter users will connect to others by following additional accounts that are of interest to the person or business (Abney, Pelletier, Ford, & Horky, 2017). The challenge with using Twitter is to create text messages that are 140 characters or less (Twitter, 2018). Hashtags are important to connect to others on this social media platform as well (Abney et al., 2017). Followers use hashtags to find information quickly (Abney et al., 2017).

An NPO can use the organization's Twitter account to raise awareness of ongoing campaigns and urgent social issues (Young, 2017). Twitter is an important social media application people refer to for current national disasters (David, Ong, & Legara, 2016; Kim, Jung, & Chilton, 2016). The more followers, the quicker current information is shared (Abney et al., 2017). The administrator of the account will need to understand and use hashtags wisely to engage others and create awareness to support the cause (Abney et al., 2017). Twitter users can easily retweet a message, adding a comment, users, and use photos to add additional information and urgency to support the cause (David et al., 2016; Kim et al., 2016).

The American Red Cross (2018) uses the NPO's Twitter account to reach out to followers and others who want to help a current cause. For example, in 2010, the American Red Cross' Twitter account shared current information of the earthquake in

Haiti (The American National Red Cross, 2018a) and in 2012, the tsunami in Japan (The American National Red Cross, 2018b). The messages included hashtags #haiti (The American National Red Cross, 2018a) and #prayforjapan (The American National Red Cross, 2018b), and a text number to immediately donate $10 (The American National Red Cross, 2018a, 2018b). The Twitter account shared images of devastation and rebuilding of significantly impacted areas, demonstrating the need and how the money donated will be used (The American National Red Cross, 2018a, 2018b). Another benefit of the Twitter account was to provide information to those in need, as to where to find shelter, food, and finding or connecting to family members (The American National Red Cross, 2018a, 2018b). The NPO raised $488 million for those in need in Haiti (The American National Red Cross, 2018a) and $312 million for those devasted by destruction in Japan (The American National Red Cross, 2018b).

The social media manager's strategy is to tweet and retweet messages, including those from senior executives (Torrealba, 2015). Messages are scheduled during the day to reach out to followers from different times zones (Torrealba, 2015). The NPO's strategy also includes the importance to share images that depict personal stories of those who helped with the donations (Torrealba, 2015). The NPO United Nations Children's Fund (UNICEF) is ranked third for the number of Twitter followers at 7.33 million, followed by TEDTalks and National Public Radio (Top Nonprofits, 2017). UNICEF ranked highest of nonprofit organizations for the number of tweets (18 per day) and retweets (184 per day) (Torrealba, 2015), maintaining an active account that reaches out to followers regularly. Tweeting and retweeting reassures donors of how the organization spends raised money to help the cause and establishes a reputation with followers and donors (Young, 2017); therefore, meets the marketing strategy of the social media manager at UNICEF.

Pinterest

The social media application Pinterest presents visual web-based pin boards, allowing users to pin images to boards from other websites or uploaded images (Pinterest, 2018b). Pinterest users can follow other accounts or specific boards of an account and receive messages of newly added pins to the followed board (Pinterest, 2018b). Followers can like, comment, and / or save pinned items to their boards (Pinterest, 2018b).

According to Omnicore Agency (2018b), women with a Pinterest account comprise of 202.5 of 250 million (81%) active Pinterest users. Qu and Steinberg (2017) concluded that women donate more to charity than men regardless of their income. An NPO marketing manager can use Pinterest to advertise with images the need for donations that can include links to its website (Qu & Steinberg, 2017).

Obvious boards and pins for The American Society for the Prevention of Cruelty to Animals (ASPCA) include pictures of animals; (a) those who were rescued, (b) those who need homes, and (c) those who need extra treatment to improve health (American Society for the Prevention of Cruelty to Animals [ASPCA], 2018, Pinterest, 2018a). The NPO's marketing manager also uses Pinterest to raise awareness of upcoming events and to demonstrate how to make donations (ASPCA, 2018; Pinterest, 2018a).

The purpose at Shelter Pet Project is to encourage people to adopt from a shelter instead of purchasing a puppy at a store (Shelter Pet Project, 2018). The Shelter Pet Project has an active Pinterest account with multiple boards based on the different types of cats and dogs available for adoption (Shelter Pet Project, 2018). Each adoptable pet image provides the user history of the animal and the shelter where it currently resides (Shelter Pet Project, 2018). Boards also include senior dogs, pets with disabilities, and stories after adoption (Shelter Pet Project, 2018). The NPO raised

$337 million dollars in advertising placements (Shelter Pet Project, 2018), essential for broadcasting to a large audience the pets in need and the importance of adopting from shelters.

Blogging

People use blogs to create a news feed with stories and images (van Esch, Aril, Castner, Talukdar, & Northey, 2018). Blogging is the only social media application that allows the marketing manager to present significant information that is not limited in characters or storage space (van Esch et al., 2018); however, the blog should be clear and concise on the message conveyed to the audience (Colton, 2018). A blog will also provide an opportunity for people to provide comments; therefore, providing instant feedback if the message is clear (Colton, 2018). A blog can provide the ability for a follower to subscribe to a new post; therefore, receiving an e-mail from updated posts (Colton, 2018).

The NPO marketing manager can use the blog to present current information with text, images, and links (Young, 2017). If the NPO has a newsletter, the NPO marketing manager could post a blog based on individual news stories presented (Young, 2017). A marketing manager can post the blog article to the NPO's Facebook page and / or Twitter account; therefore, reaching out to a larger social media audience (Young, 2017). The NPO marketing manager has the ability to facilitate conversations with people interested in the NPO, as long as the blog post is set up to allow comments from donors or potential supporters (Young, 2017).

The American Lebanese Syrian Associated Charities (ALSAC) conducts fundraising campaigns and received donations for the St. Jude Children's Research Hospital (St. Jude Children's Research Hospital, 2018b). The marketing team of ALSAC uses the St. Jude website to host the program, St. Jude Blogger Ambassadors program (St. Jude Children's Research Hospital, 2018a). The purpose of the program is to encourage people who are familiar with the work at St. Jude, and the families of children who were medically treated and healed (St. Jude Children's Research Hospital, 2018a). Stories shared from posting blogs on a central website, depict the success and gratefulness of donations made to the organization (St. Jude Children's Research Hospital, 2018a).

Instagram

The social media application Instagram was introduced in 2010 (Abbott, Donaghey, Hare, & Hopkins, 2013). The main use of this social media platform is a visual message with shared photos and/or videos with the mobile app (Abbott et al., 2013), as opposed to text messages on Facebook and Twitter. According to Omnicore Agency (2018), the company hosts 600 million active users. The user can easily share a post on Instagram to the Facebook and Twitter account; therefore, sending one message to multiple social media applications (Abbott et al., 2013).

The primary purpose to use Instagram as a social media marketing tool is to share images rather than text messages (Abbott et al., 2013). Consumers share images of using products or services and tag the company for recognition and endorsement (Virtanen, Bjork, & Sjostrom, 2017). The marketing manager of the company should in return, reply to the tagged image (Virtanen et al., 2017). Followers of the original posts will see the interaction between consumer and company marketer; therefore, intriguing interests in following a company that takes the time to build relationships with its customers (Abbott et al., 2013).

In 2016, World Bicycle Relief began a marketing campaign *Together We Rise* (World Bicycle Relief, 2017). The purpose of this fundraiser was to raise money and awareness for the need to provide bicycles to children in developing countries (World Bicycle Relief, 2017). The NPO used Instagram to provide visuals for the need of donations and bicycles, such as the children productively using the donated bicycles (World Bicycle Relief, 2017). In 2017, the company surpassed its goal, providing 1,617 bicycles based on the Twitter #GivingTuesday and *Together We Rise campaign* (World Bicycle Relief, 2017).

Pencils of Promise is an NPO to raise money for children who are unable to receive an education due to poverty (Pencils of Promise, 2018a). The marketing manager regularly changes the profile on the Instagram account to the current fundraiser (Pencils of Promise, 2018b). This information provides donors easy access to submit a donation (Pencils of Promise, 2018b). Pictures of happy children, recipient of donations to classrooms and thank you note images to those who contributed to the cause confirms the money is going to a good cause and the organization is making a difference for children in need (Pencils of Promise, 2018b). Pencils of Promise built 481 schools that hold 94,241 students as of 2018, with the donations provided through social media strategies that include the main use of Instagram (Pencils of Promise, 2018b).

YouTube

The social media platform YouTube is a video-sharing website for users to create a channel to store videos (Legewie & Nassauer, 2018). Google owns YouTube, the most common search engine used globally; therefore, creates a larger audience for viewing (Legewie & Nassauer, 2018). This site provides closed captioning and sharing to other social media applications, such as Facebook and Twitter (Legewie & Nassauer, 2018).

Several NPOs used YouTube for successful marketing campaigns, such as Big Brothers Big Sisters, charitable: water, March of Dimes, and Make-A-Wish Foundation (YouTube, 2018). According to Arthurs, Drakopoulou, and Gandini (2018), YouTube is the second most visited website with 4 billion videos uploaded on the social media application by 2016. Dehghani, Niaki, Ramezani, and Sali (2016) confirmed marketing campaigns on YouTube create awareness of the company brand, mission, vision, and purpose. Videos should include the staff, volunteers, customers, and donors in action (Waters & Jones, 2011).

Founded in 1904, the Big Brother Big Sisters of America nonprofit began years before social media existed (Big Brother Big Sisters of America, 2018a). In 2011, the NPO began a Be a Part of Something BIG campaign; a movement that presents videos on YouTube to depict the NPO's volunteers' success stories and the need for donations to continue serving the communities' children without parents and/or siblings (Big Brother Big Sisters of America, 2018b). The marketing manager measures the success of the campaign by the number of views per video; an average of 5,000 views per message (Big Brother Big Sisters of America, 2018b).

NPO charitable: water successfully uses YouTube for presenting videos that capture the organization's messages from its founder, the purpose of the organization (mission, vision, and values), and action in the community (charitable: water, 2018). Allowing the organization's staff to express their gratitude for donors and support created the most successful marketing campaign of the NPO (Charitable: Water, 2018). This social media campaign generated $42 million dollars used to serve 2 million people in need of clean, drinkable water (charitable: water, 2018).

Multiple Social Media Applications

Using one social media application wisely can provide many benefits to the NPO (Fudurić & Mandelli, 2017). The ability to use multiple social media applications can prove more rewarding; however, a social media strategy should be in writing to ensure meeting of the goals of the NPO (Fudurić & Mandelli, 2017). Depending on the size of the NPO and the staff to run the marketing campaigns, will determine if there is a need and ability to use and monitor more than one social media application (Fuduri & Mandelli, 2017). Jones and Daniel (2018) concluded people prefer different social media platforms for different reasons and uses. If an NPO's social media strategy includes more than one social media application, the chances of reaching out to more donors are likely (Jones & Daniels, 2018).

The March of Dimes uses blogging, Facebook, YouTube, and Twitter to send information about the organization's mission, vision, and charitable needs (March of Dimes, 2018). The multiple social media platforms ensure the information reaches the targeted audience with clear messages in text, visuals, and videos (Fuduri & Mandelli, 2017). In 2017, the NPO raised $108 million at events marketed on the various social media accounts (March of Dimes, 2018). The money provided health care for babies and mothers (March of Dimes, 2018).

Discussion

There are several social media applications available that are free to use and can be used as a marketing platform to send messages about the NPO's mission, vision, purpose, and campaigns (Agozzino & Fleck, 2016; Feng et al., 2017; Waters & Jones, 2011). The most popular and proven used successfully are Facebook, Twitter, Pinterest, blogging, Instagram, and YouTube (Casale, 2015; Statista, 2018). A social media strategy is successful only if the account is active and regularly monitored, preferably by a marketing expert (Feng et al., 2017). The social media strategy should provide a plan that ensures the mission, vision, purpose, and goals of the NPO is met (Agozzino & Fleck, 2016; Feng et al., 2017; Waters & Jones, 2011). The social media strategy can also include other targets for accomplishments, such as fundraising, brand building, and reputation management (Feng et al., 2017).

Understanding the target audience could help determine the best social media applications to use (Feng et al., 2017; Jones & Daniels, 2017). The marketing manager will need to confirm if one or multiple social media platforms are needed to get the message out to the appropriate people (Fudurić & Mandelli, 2017). Tracking the social media account can ensure the social media strategy is effective and meeting the needs and goals of the NPO (Agozzino et al., 2016; Feng et al., 2017; Fudurić & Mandelli, 2017; Tafesse & Wien, 2018).

Conclusion

The benefits of social media applications exist for NPOs; therefore, a written social media strategy should be a priority of the NPO leader and / or marketing manager. The social media strategy may include marketing messaging on Facebook, Twitter, Pinterest, blogging, Instagram, or YouTube. The social media plan can include one or multiple social media applications. The Refractive Thinker® considers making good business decisions based on successful social media strategies to create a better chance of marketing success and consumer satisfaction to donate to the NPO.

THOUGHTS FROM THE ACADEMIC ENTREPRENEUR

The problem to be solved:

- What social media strategies are available and successful to attract donors

The goals:

- Understanding the strategies a marketing manager can implement to create a social media
- Presenting success stories of social media strategies successfully used by NPOs

The questions to ask:

- What social media applications will provide a marketing platform to generate donations and information about the nonprofit?
- Should the social media strategy include more than one social media application?

Today's Business Application:

- A written social media strategy should be a priority for the NPO leaders and / or marketing manager.
- Active social media accounts can depict the need for donations and demonstrate the success of donations.

REFERENCES

Abbott, W., Donaghey, J., Hare, J., & Hopkins, P. (2013). An Instagram is worth a thousand words: An industry panel and audience Q & A. *Library Hi Tech News, 30*(7), 1-6. doi:10.1108/LHTN-08-2013-0047

Abney, A. K., Pelletier, M. J., Ford, T. S., & Horky, A. B. (2017). #IHateYourBrand: Adaptive service recovery strategies on Twitter. *The Journal of Services Marketing, 31*(3), 281-294. doi:10.1108/JSM-02-2016-0079

Agozzino, A., & Fleck, K. R. (2016). Examining nonprofit strategy for fundraising on a social media platform: A content analysis of top 10 U.S. nonprofit power brands fundraising efforts on Facebook. *Public Relations Journal, 10*, 1-33. Retrieved from https://prjounral.instituteforpr.org

American Society for the Prevention of Cruelty to Animals (ASPCA). (2018). *ASPCApro. New on Pinterest: Behavior board for dogs.* Retrieved from https://www.aspcapro.org/blog/2016/10/27/new-pinterest-behavior-board-dogs

Arthurs, J., Drakopoulou, S., & Gandini, A. (2018). Researching YouTube. *Convergence: The International Journal of Research into New Media Technologies, 24*(1), 3-15. doi:10.1177/1354856517737222

Big Brothers Big Sisters of America. (2018a). *About us.* Retrieved from http://www.bbbs.org/about-us

Big Brothers Big Sisters of America. (2018b). *Be a part of something big.* Retrieved from http://www.bbbs.org/donate

Casale, N. (2015). *Generational preferences in marketing medium selections of animal adoptions in nonprofit organizations: A correlational study* (Doctoral dissertation). Retrieved from ProQuest Digital Dissertations and Theses database. (UMI No. 3708595)

charitable: water. (2018). *How we work.* Retrieved from https://www.charitywater.org/projects

Colton, D. A. (2018). Antecedents of consumer attitudes' toward corporate blogs. *Journal of Research in Interactive Marketing, 12*(1), 94-104. doi:10.1108/JRIM-08-2017-0075

David, C. C., Ong, J. C., & Legara, E. F. (2016). Tweeting super-typhoon Haiyan: Evolving functions of Twitter during and after a disaster event. *PLoS ONE, 11*(3), 1-19. doi:10.1371.journal.pone/0150190

Dehghani, M., Niaki, M. K., Ramezani, I., & Sali, R. (2016). Evaluating the influence of YouTube advertising for attraction of your customers. *Computers in Human Behavior, 59*(C), 165-172. doi:10.1016/j.chb.2016.01.037

Feng, Y., Du, L., & Ling, Q. (2017). How social media strategies of nonprofit organizations affect consumer donation intention and word-of-mouth.

Social Behavior and Personality: An International Journal, 45, 1775-1786. doi:10.2224/sbp.4412

Fudurić, M., & Mandelli, A. (2017). Corporate and non-profit social media policies: A content analysis. *Trziste Market, 29*(1), 7-22. doi:10.22598/mt/2017.29.1.7

Jones, J. A., & Daniel, D. L. (2018). A method for research and practice: Using a developmentally informed interview to increase donor engagement. *The Journal of Nonprofit Education and Leadership, 8*(2), 182-195. doi:10.18666/JNEL-2018-V8-I2-8723

Kim, J., & Yu, E. A. (2016). The holistic brand experience of branded mobile applications affects brand loyalty. *Social Behavior and Personality, 44*(1), 77-87. doi:10.2224/sbp.2016.44.1.77

Kim, K., Jung, K., & Chilton. K. (2016). Strategies of social media use in disaster management. *International Journal of Emergency Services, 5*(2), 110-125. doi:10.1108/IJES-02-2016-0005

Legewie, N., & Nassauer, A. (2018). YouTube, Google, Facebook: 21 century online video research and research ethics. *Qualitative Social Research, 19*(3), 1-19. doi:10.17169/fqs-19.3.3130

March of Dimes. (2018). *Annual report.* Retrieved from https://www.marchofdimes.org/mission/annual-report.aspx

Musonera, E., & Weber, J. M. (2018). Analysis of marketing strategies in the social media: Facebook case analysis. *Journal of Marketing Development and Competitiveness, 12*(1), 10-27. Retrieved from http://www.na-businesspress.com/JMDC

National Council of Nonprofits. (2018). *Nonprofit impact in communities.* Retrieved from http://www.councilofnonprofits.org/nonprofit-impact-communities

Nonprofit Tech for Good. (2018). *2018 Global NGO technology report.* Retrieved from https://www.techreport.ngo

Omnicore Agency. (2018a). *Instagram by the numbers: Stats, demographics & fun facts.* Retrieved from https://www.omnicoreagency.com/instagram-statistics

Omnicore Agency. (2018b). *Pinterest by the numbers: Stats, demographics & fun facts.* Retrieved from https://www.omnicoreagency.com/pinterest-statistics

Pelletier, M. J., & Horky, A. B. (2015). Exploring the Facebook like: A product and service perspective. *Journal of Research in Interactive Marketing, 9,* 337-354. doi:10.1108/JRIM-09-2014-0059

Pencils of Promise. (2018a). *About us. Everyone has promise.* Retrieved from https://pencilsofpromise.org/about

Pencils of Promise. (2018b). *Our work: How we track our progress.* Retrieved from https://pencilsofpromise.org/results

Pew Research Center. (2018). *U.S. labor force by generation, 1995–2015.* Retrieved from https://www.pewresearch.org/fact-ank/2018/04/11/millennials-largest-generation-us-labor-force/ft_15-05-04_genlaborforcecomposition-2/

Pinterest. (2018a). *ASPCA.* Retrieved from https://www.pinterest.com/ASPCA

Pinterest. (2018b). *How Pinterest works.* Retrieved from https://business.pinterest.com/en/how-pinterest-works

Qu, H., & Steinberg, R. (2017). Charitable giving in nonprofit service associations: Identities, incentives, and gender differences. *Nonprofit and Voluntary Sector Quarterly, 46,* 984-1005. doi:10.1177/0899764017703709

Shelter Pet Project. (2018). *About our campaign.* Retrieved from https://theshelterpetproject.org/about-our-campaign

Statista. (2018). *Social media sites and tools used by U.S. charity and nonprofit organizations as of 2014.* Retrieved from https://www.statista.com/statistics/310006/us-charity-and-non-profit-social-media-usage/

St. Jude Children's Research Hospital. (2018a). *St. Jude blogger ambassadors.* Retrieved from https://www.stjude.org/get-involved/other-ways/blogger-ambassadors.html

St. Jude Children's Research Hospital. (2018b). *What's ALSAC?* Retrieved from https://www.stjude.org/about-st-jude/faq/whats-alsac.html

Tafesse, W., & Wien, A. (2018). Using message strategy to drive consumer behavioral engagement on social media. *Journal of Consumer Marketing, 35*(3), 241-253. doi:10.1108/JCM-08-2016-1905

The ALS Association. (2018). *ALS ice bucket challenge–FAQ.* Retrieved from http://www.alsa.org/about-us/ice-bucket-challenge-faq.html

The American National Red Cross. (2018a). *American Red Cross in Haiti.* Retrieved from https://www.redcross.org/about-us/our-work/international-services/haiti-assistance-program.html

The American National Red Cross. (2018b). *On the path to recovery Japan earthquake and tsunami.* Retrieved from https://www.redcross.org/content/dam/redcross/atg/PDFs/Reports/ARC_Japan_Year2_R3.pdf

Top Nonprofits. (2017). *Top nonprofits on Twitter.* Retrieved from https://www.topnonprofits.com/lists/top-nonprofits-on-twitter

Torrealba, A. A. (2015). Twiplomacy: Impact of Twitter social network on diplomacy. *Vestnik Rudn. 15*(3), 152-166. Retrieved from http://journals/rudn.ru/international-relations

Twitter, Inc. (2018). *Ad targeting.* Retrieved from https://business.twitter.com/en/targeting.html

YouTube impact lab: Campaigns. (2018). Retrieved from https://www.youtube.com/yt/impactlab/campaigns/

van Esch, P., Aril, D., Castner, J., Talukdar, N., & Northey, G. (2018). Consumer attitudes towards bloggers and paid blog advertisements: what's new? *Marketing Intelligence & Planning, 36*, 778-793. doi:10.1108/MIP-01-2018-0027

Vinerean, S. (2017). Importance of strategic social media marketing. *Expert Journal of Marketing, 5*(1), 28-35. Retrieved from https://www.marketing.expertjournals.com

Virtanen, H., Bjork, P., & Sjostrom, E. (2017). Follow for follow: Marketing of a start-up company on Instagram. *Journal of Small Business and Enterprise Development, 24*, 468-484. doi:10.1108/JSBED-12-2016-0202

Waters, R. D., & Jones, P. M. (2011). Using video to build an organization's identity and brand: A content analysis of nonprofit organizations' YouTube videos. *Journal of Nonprofit & Public Sector Marketing, 23*(3), 248-268. doi:10.1080/10495142.2011.594779

World Bicycle Relief. (2017). *Our biggest #GIVINGTUESDAY yet!* Retrieved from https://worldbicyclerelief.org/en/giving-tuesday-2017/

Young, J. A. (2017). Facebook, Twitter, and blogs: The adoption and utilization of social media in nonprofit human service organizations. *Human Service Organizations, Management, Leadership, & Governance, 41*(1), 44-57. doi:10.1080/23303131.2016.1192574

About the Author...

Dr. Natalie Casale resides in Little Silver, New Jersey. Dr. Natalie holds several accredited degrees: a Bachelor of Science (BS) in Information Technology from Kean University, a Master of Business Administration (MBA) in Accounting from Monmouth University, and a Doctorate of Management (DM) in Organizational Leadership from the University of Phoenix School of Advanced Studies. Dr. Natalie is a fulltime university professor and associate online chair with Berkeley College, and part-time faculty with the University of Phoenix and Walden University. Dr. Natalie serves as a dissertation mentor / chair and committee member.

Dr. Natalie is a member of the University of Phoenix Lambda Sigma Chapter of the International Business Honor Society, Delta Mu Delta (DMD). Dr. Natalie is a volunteer National and New Jersey State District Leader of the Humane Society of the United States (HSUS) and recognized community leaders in animal welfare.

To reach Dr. Natalie Casale, please visit her **website:** http://www.nataliecasale.com or **e-mail:** nataliecasale@mac.com

CHAPTER 2

What Nonprofit Organizations Need to Unlearn

Dr. Julee H. Hafner

How can leaders within Nonprofit Organizations (NPOs) unlearn to effectively update knowledge during environmental change? In this chapter, the lens of basic organizational fundamentals develops an understanding of factors that characterize individual unlearning within the non-profit sector. Since Hedberg (1981), organizational unlearning continues to gain more attention, although this topic in the literature still lags behind organizational learning. Unlearning is a true refractive thinking process where this type of innovation can facilitate new ways to think and solve current organizational challenges.

This chapter speaks to the implications of maintaining skill competency value during knowledge change within the non-profit sector where true refractive thinkers can focus for desired outcomes. The objectives for Chapter 2 are to understand the importance of knowledge as a valuable resource and to describe the process for updating skills to reduce negative organizational effects. Decreased productivity, reduced quality, and additional costs are examples of unintended consequences of failure to unlearn and change (Leibowitz, 2000).

The ability to maintain competitive advantage becomes difficult for organizations and individuals when knowledge grows exponentially. According to Starkey, Tempest, and McKlinay (2004), "In the global economy, knowledge is king," and "in such an environment, knowledge counts for more than capital or labor"

(p. 74). Organizations need to use innovative strategies to maximize the impact of the knowledge they possess. Knowledge or a knowledge base is the aggregate of information that a worker can acquire and use through experience, study, or understanding of a particular subject (Becker, 2007).

NPOs are not unique in their effort to develop solutions to solve problems. NPOs focus on service, whereas for-profit organizations (FPOs) goals are to make profits for stockholders, however, both organizations need to raise revenue and reduce costs for their functions and sustainability. This chapter will use the term *associate* to refer to individuals who work and volunteer for NPOs, while the term *employees* will refer to an FPO worker.

Leaders add technology and processes to solve problems using an ever-expanding knowledge base. Unlearning, knowledge acquisition and modification, might involve a replacement of prior knowledge (Hedberg, 1981). The implications are that global organizations depend upon consistent knowledge management practices to maintain a competitive advantage (Akgün, Byrne, Lynn, & Keskin, 2007; Tsang, & Zahra, 2008). The difficulty arises when managers must create the modifications in processes, procedures, actions, and behaviors in employees to update skills (Becker, 2011, 2004; Nystrom & Starbuck, 2011). NPOs need techniques to expand and maintain market share while retaining the knowledge base they possess no matter how the core of personnel changes. Knowledge change, updating, or modification of skill competencies is more than difficult than initially thought.

The Practical Problem

It was common for a worker to learn a set of skills that would last during his or her occupational lifetime in the 1900s (Clark, 2010). Workers play a key role in the implementation of current information, and competencies during job task performance.

However, with the need to update skills especially since the 2000s, individuals might have a challenge in modifying, storing, and using new information to complete a job function when the previously learned function is no longer valid (Clark, 2010). Without continual modifications to maintain skill competency, the amount of wasted time, additional energy, and resources required will continue to increase at an alarming rate. To reduce these impacts, systemic change through unlearning is necessary (Leape & Berwick, 2005). Organizations will require updating to be sustainable.

Organizations with the ability to manage the precious resource of associate knowledge will be far ahead of those that only manage tangible items such as goods or services (Nonaka, 1994). The organizations and individuals who have the capacity to understand these knowledge shifts and change processes will have an advantage over those who do not (Nonaka, 1994; Starkey, Tempest, & McKinlay, 2004). Innovative thinking during knowledge change becomes important to organizations that are dependent on the capital of knowledge. Using knowledge as a resource can prove important to NPOs who are undergoing change. Strategies to improve knowledge economics, such as unlearning are worth investigating.

To have the ability to acquire knowledge and use individual intellectual capital are important organizational resources to survive in changing conditions (Leibowitz & Beckman, 1998). Marketplace shifts, regulatory, and technological advances all impact the success potential of either FPOs or NPOs. Unfortunately, using the sum total of organizational knowledge often remains an underutilized resource as more up to date information is acquired.

The NPO Dilemma

Leaders of NPOs and FPOs could learn much from each other about how to manage the impact of knowledge change and its importance to skill competencies for marketplace sustainability. FPOs function to maximize profits to return them to the company's owners and shareholders, whereas NPOs such as, Boys & Girls Clubs of America or Disabled American Veterans Charitable Service Trust function to satisfy a need within society. However, as changes within society and resource scarcity occur, NPOs must forge new pathways to maximize their operational revenue and update their business strategies.

When environment conditions change, all organizations must update their skills, competencies, and capacity for change, or they will not remain sustainable. Developing strategies to reduce re-work, errors, and costs can benefit both types of organizations. Factors for facilitating knowledge change, or unlearning, can provide innovative training methodologies that help associates adopt new actions.

All organizations need to understand knowledge change process techniques to remain competitive and sustainable. NPO processes and procedures can be comparable to organizations within the FPO sector but are changing for several reasons. The increasing impact of the knowledge explosion impacts FPO success however, these impacts often go unnoticed in the non-profit sector. Because additional environmental shifts occur, an increase in the sheer number of new FPO businesses competing with NPOs have altered the landscape and safety of previously held marketplaces. FPOs are concentrating resources and interests in social change with products and services that have a benefit to the disadvantaged. Social change was previously a specialized focus of the NPO, adding another competitor to the environment.

Last, as investor concerns over issues of ethical behavior and producing a return in societal change, NPOs accountability for the invested capital are the norm. The NPO can no longer just provide for the greater good, they must maintain financial solvency, and meet benchmarks while providing solutions to societies' problems.

NPOs need to modify outdated business practices. Technological advances streamline work processes, regulatory and fiscal changes reduce avenues of governmental support, and new for-profit companies entered into markets traditionally held by NPOs, continuing to impact NPO success (Topaloglu, McDonald, & Hunt, 2018). This new dynamic and global business environment change is standard for FPOs with NPOs following suit. Unfortunately, change remains difficult.

To this end, NPOs continue to add for-profit structures and processes, to not only maximize revenue, but to grow. One such example, is Special Olympics, which has seen dramatic growth of 8% in 2010 serving over 3.37 million athletes (Kessler, 2011). The Chief Executive Officer (CEO), Tim Shriver, suggested that when change is eminent, an organization needs to unlearn previous knowledge to make their business processes thrive, which he feels is a major change within the nonprofit sector. Special Olympics have unlearned the idea of institutionalization in favor of fighting exclusion and nonproductive attitudes. Metrics have focused on attitude change to innovate and increase impact (Kessler, 2011).

Additionally, educational personnel undergo to technological change requiring unlearning of old knowledge. Reassessment of old routines and processes is needed to provide accountability, reach goals, and provide instruction of new knowledge. Implementing change might involve using new ways to perform in the classroom (Schaffer, 2007). When a teacher updates an existing process, adoption of change includes, allowing time to experiment and discover where the knowledge gaps are, facilitation of the change process occurs. Successful unlearning is achieved by those who adopt updated knowledge (Noteboom & Hafner, 2015b).

NPOs continue to try to gain expertise from FPOs because FPOs have been able to weather more changes in the market environment (Kessler, 2011). Many organizations consider themselves *learning* and use new processes to train, maintain skill competency, and share knowledge within their organizations. Associates in the knowledge economy, must possess specialized skills to be innovators, make rapid changes in the fast and flexible environment, and assist in meeting organizational benchmarks. FPOs such as Hewlett-Packard and Coca Cola attempted to improve their skill competencies by capturing and sharing knowledge (Leibowitz, 2000). A survey of these Fortune 500 companies indicated only 4 out of 200 companies consider themselves knowledge organizations and are only beginning to realize the value of employee knowledge.

Additionally, organizations need to strengthen their ability to use knowledge productively to maintain mission, vision, and values today and into the future (Becker, 2007, 2011). Understanding the process of unlearning might positively impact the organization's ability to acquire, update and adopt new knowledge. Organizations can remain competitive by identifying those that are able to meet the challenges with technological ease and adopt updated knowledge. Research points the way to identifying unlearning characteristics and facilitators that can improve training processes in all organizations.

Rapid shifts in current organizational and individual knowledge base is essential to performing organizational tasks, avoiding errors, and re-work is essential to keeping operating costs in check while maintaining excellent goods and services (Rushmer & Davies, 2004). As the amount of information within an organization increases, knowledge is increasingly more difficult to manage. This knowledge base represents all the knowledge an organization possess, and the knowledge that each individual employee or associate that works for the NPO or FPO possesses. Associate skill competencies are lost when they leave the organization. Associate knowledge that remain true to the mission, vision, and values is a valuable resource because individual knowledge is hard to recapture once lost. Understanding how to manage knowledge is essential to organizations. Individual intellectual capital can serve the organization's success if they facilitate the process (Kong & Ferrell, 2010). When an NPO fails to understand the value of their intellectual capital, they lose their advantage and organizational failure might result (Starkey et al., 2004).

FPOs have sought solutions to produce consistent, competent skills while updating organizational processes. NPOs will be also be charged with finding similar effective learning change practices in the new knowledge economy. A traditional method of learning change used strategies of identifying gaps in knowledge and teaching lacking information to close gaps. Faulty learning completion where knowledge gaps remain yield decreased work product quality, and productivity, or increased product costs, let alone the personal cost to employees who must replace prior knowledge.

Knowledge Change Perspectives

Literature on the process of unlearning traces its roots in the 1980s (Hedberg, 1981). However, advances in the study of knowledge management and acquisition have developed a new interest about unlearning (Leape & Berwick, 2005). Researchers have a new interest in unlearning due to its importance and application in maintaining skill competencies and facilitating the alteration of knowledge with unlearning appearing in many disciplines (Becker, 2007). Understanding the unlearning process can facilitate the creation and alteration of knowledge for any organizational framework (Becker, 2011).

The acquisition, refinement, and updating of basic competency presents an ongoing problem for organizations (Becker, 2011; Cegarra-Navarro & Moya, 2005; Leibowitz, 2000). Organizations with the ability to manage the precious resource of knowledge will be far ahead of those who do not (Rushmer & Davies, 2004). Implementation of new processes within an organization might result in the potential to increase work product errors, creating technological upset (Hafner, 2014; 2015). Knowledge advances create a need to unlearn old competencies. Without skill competency maintenance, employees might expend additional time and energy, increasing service delivery costs while noting a decrease in job satisfaction. Unlike learning, that involves new skill or knowledge acquisition, unlearning, replaces knowledge, action, or procedures when appropriate by substituting new knowledge (Hedberg, 1981). Unlearning adds validated, updated knowledge, when new data is added, and might be a part of the learning process (Hafner, 2014; Starbuck, 1996).

Organizations need to understand the components of successful unlearning in order to focus on updating associate practices. Upgrading procedures and processes to new ones are commonplace in today's global economy. For example, in the development of new technology, there is a need to replace machines with newer versions that more closely support service delivery functions. Many of the users develop unconscious or rote behavior when working with a particular technology (Wood & Neal, 2016; Wood, Tam, & Witt, 2005). When making changes, users are required to revise their mental models and actions when using new versions of equipment. Facilitating the change process, through unlearning is key. Facilitation methods include, developing awareness and discovery of knowledge gaps, experimentation of new procedures, and having additional support of other associates who are also updating skills.

During transformational learning of a new competency, employees use previously acquired knowledge until new knowledge becomes available. To utilize newly acquired knowledge, old processes become outdated and require replacement, making way for emerging new processes, skills and competencies (Senge, 2006; Starbuck, 1996). The organizational member produces change using additional knowledge processing and stabilization (Schmorrow, Cohn, & Nicholson, 2010; Senge, 2006; Starbuck, 1996). Automatic actions, behaviors, and *mental models* are altered through the process of *unlearning* (Becker, 2011; Hedberg, 1981; Senge, 2006). Whether the individual has control over change or it is an unconscious activity process remains unaccounted for during unlearning (Clark, 2010). Research indicated the present knowledge base and individual learning style impacts competency, but these processes might also impact unlearning (Hafner, 2014).

Organizations are affected in their product or service quality, and additional operating costs might result (Becker, 2008). When individual unlearning is unsuccessful, production of errors can occur, creating increased confusion and tension in associates (Hafner, 2014; Hafner & Noteboom, 2015b). Errors might consist of slow, incorrect, or inconsistent actions. Types of errors could include, omissions of data, interruptions in learning behavior, and incomplete or faulty updating of skill competencies (Hafner, 2016; Reeler, 2001).

Unlearning continues to be an important, although a poorly understood part of the learning cycle, however, there remains no clear consensus about this process (Becker, 2004). Newstrom (1983) posited individuals begin with a *clean slate* before adding information. The brain would actually erase unneeded information (Low, 2011). Clark (2010) discounted this concept as faulty, as this would require storage and processing capabilities exceeding the capacity of the brain.

However, all associates require the realization that previous knowledge is unreliable, and they need to stop using it (Neal et al., 2012; Starbuck, 1996). Realization initiates knowledge updating and can be from an external source such as, when an organization selects a new version of a computer system or application for associate to use to complete a job function. Internal forces when information or actions previously used are no longer valid can also initiate learning change.

Bloom's (1956) taxonomy provides a foundation using three domains for the process of knowledge acquisition: (a) the affective,

(b) the psychomotor, and (c) the cognitive domain (Bloom & Krathwohl, 1956). In this paper, the affective domain focuses on the way the learner responds to knowledge, and the psychomotor domain focuses on how the learner performs the actions of a task. Learning of factual knowledge and recall are present in the cognitive domain (Bloom & Krathwohl, 1956).

Nystrom and Starbuck (2011) suggested that the idea that an individual should "eliminate preexisting knowledge or habits that would otherwise represent formidable barriers to new learning" (p. 36), but this theory remains unconfirmed. When employees have unlearned previously used knowledge to update their knowledge base, knowledge might be absorbed, but not necessarily used (Wheatley, 2006). Acquiring and changing skill competencies from previously acquired knowledge base can be difficult, resulting in confusions and technological upset while new knowledge is tested (Hafner, 2014; Nissen, 2006; Nonaka & von Krogh, 2009).

Griswold and Kaiser (2017), theoretically suggested that disequilibrium in previously held routines will reduce old influencers. When an individual is in the process of change, knowledge might be selected for change. These behaviors are intentionally discarded to become a better version self; however, this implies unlearning is entirely under cognitive control (Griswold & Kaiser, 2017). Clark (2010) presented several open statements and unresolved problems about unlearning: (a) Adults are largely unaware of the strategies of how they acquire and change knowledge, (b) the role of interference from habit or cognitive behaviors might impact change, and (c) how dysfunctional unconscious knowledge is unlearned remains unknown.

Unlearning involves both a change in the previously learned knowledge base and how the brain changes old unconscious behaviors within the knowledge base into new automatic behaviors (Hafner, 2014; Schmorrow et al., 2010). Consistency in repetition, knowledge storage, and retrieval systems need to be in place, for a complete unlearning process to occur where knowledge base is formed (Ouellette & Wood, 1998; Schmorrow et al., 2010). Discarding current competencies and mental models in favor of the new knowledge takes awareness, consistency, and stabilization until the action is easily used (Leape & Berwick, 2005; Starbuck, 1998). However, successful, consistent behavioral repetition within an environment is required (Schmorrow et al., 2010; Tsang & Zahra, 2008). When unlearning is unsuccessful, errors in processes might result. Data that are no longer reliable, might not be integrated into existing skill competencies, and a state of flux is created.

An example would be when there are advances in technology and updating is required to complete job functions. From an organizational learning perspective, Attewell (1992) defined technology assimilation as "a process of organizational learning in which individuals and an organization as a whole acquire the knowledge and skills necessary to effectively apply the technology" (p. 1345). The burden of unlearning creates a knowledge barrier that might inhibit diffusion of information. When an associate has any barrier to adoption of a new system, it is because there needs to be an awareness of a knowledge gap and desire to adopt the new system. Understanding unlearning will prove useful, especially when NPOs want to add successful frameworks to their organizational strategies.

Research indicated that unlearning involves more than just the replacement of knowledge (Wheatley, 2006). Study data from several related studies have yielded important information about the unlearning process. In the initial study, *Unlearning in Organizational Employees*, the organization initiated a need for a knowledge change (Hafner, 2014). Employees from a midsized engineering organization were interviewed about their perceptions of knowledge change, unlearning. Employees acknowledged their previous actions were unreliable and they needed to stop using them. The employees needed to unlearn previous actions to initiate new more productive ones and change the previous knowledge base. Employees reported difficulty with the process (Hafner, 2014). Frustration appeared as the predominant comment. Employees noted an emotional upset that unbalanced their competency and their knowledge to the complete job tasks. This result is certainly possible in an NPO.

When creating an effective knowledge process, errorless task performance is a key objective (Rushmer & Davies, 2004). Healthcare organizations need speed and accuracy in service delivery. When processes change, service providers are required to update current knowledge base skills as a routine scope of practice. Surveyed healthcare practitioners responded to be successful, with a realization of a gap in their knowledge between old and new skills. A comparison of the knowledge inconsistencies occurred, and updated information filled this gap. When practitioners were unable to make the changes because of the difficulties with the process or perceived the updated process to have a limited benefit for the practitioner, change was not likely to occur (Hafner, 2016; Hafner & Noteboom, 2015; Noteboom, Hafner, & Wahbeha, 2017). Healthcare participants reported feelings of confusion and tension creating a type of upset. Adoption of a new knowledge base is not easy when other practitioners negative perceptions detract from the process.

Perceptions of unlearning during hearing instrument technology advances were surveyed. Hearing aid practitioners reported when the technology was intuitive, easy to learn, and there was some benefit to making changes, practitioners reported technological ease. A positive environment allowed additional time for changes to occur, experimentation with new knowledge, and support during their change facilitated unlearning. Respondents noted successful, complete unlearning occurred and resulted in an effective useable knowledge base.

According to Miller, West, Brown, Sim, and Ganchoff (2005), achieving healthcare quality improvements through Electronic Medical Records system (EMRs) depends on a physicians' use of the EMRs for daily tasks. However, the implementation of new technologies, such as EMRs, generates internal problems, especially when there are conflicts with current structure and routines (Cegarra-Navarro & Cepeda, 2013; Cegarra-Navarro & Dewhurst, 2006; Cegarra-Navarro & Moya, 2005). When looking at the ability for unlearning in healthcare organizations, we do not know why some physicians intuitively learn (the EMR) while others encounter various levels of difficulties.

Rethinking of the traditional views about healthcare are characterized along two main unlearning themes- complete / successful and incomplete / unsuccessful unlearning. Data analysis indicated that the introduction of new Health Information Technologies (HITs), such as EMRs, affect the unlearning process positively and negatively at the same time. Complete unlearning positively impacted the physicians' work practices by facilitating the unlearning processes and establishing comfort and ease with EMR (Hafner & Noteboom, 2015a; Hafner & Noteboom, 2015b).

Physicians reported, when working with an EMR system that was more difficult, they felt technological upset (Hafner & Noteboom, 2015b). Changes to practitioner knowledge base were more difficult due to the design of the system and the systems' non-intuitiveness. Decreased physician collaboration was perceived because of unsupported functions, such as when ordering drugs from the pharmacy and lack of system interfaces between various specialties, clinics, or providers. When physicians adopted the EMR, they had fewer difficulties and appeared more at ease with the unlearning process. Their understanding of new patient care processes and the perceptions of competency helped them work more effectively with the new EMR system (Hafner & Noteboom, 2015a; Noteboom, Hafner, & Wahbeha, 2017).

Unfortunately, incomplete unlearning negatively impacted the physicians' work practices and workflows. The EMR system made physicians frustrated, reduced collaboration with patients and co-workers, and established upset and poor adoption of new technology. The present knowledge base and individual unlearning ability impacted competency. Incomplete unlearning is defined as, "inconsistency in repetition, knowledge storage, and retrieval systems in place" (Hafner, 2016, p. 4325) reducing effectiveness of knowledge change. A adapted summary model of the process of unlearning is in Figure 1 (Hafner, 2014).

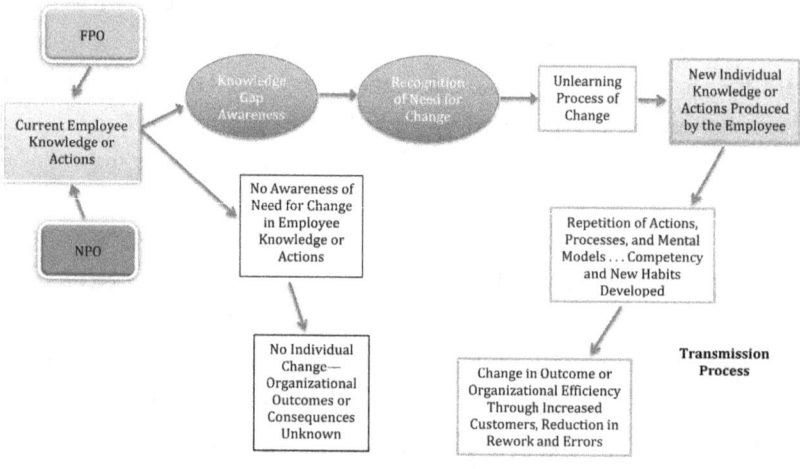

Figure 1. Unlearning Process Model

In this unlearning process model (see Figure 1), both NPOs and FPOs use the same process to complete their knowledge change process to achieve organizational goals and remain competitive. As the awareness that incorrect and outdated processes are recognized, change must occur. The worker, through experimentation and discovery is able to make incremental modifications of individual competencies and procedures to complete a task in a new way. Through repetition, a new knowledge or skill is reproduced, with enough frequency that knowledge is stabilized and a new competency is formed. Change has occurred, resulting in new organizational outcomes.

When any organization wants to make a knowledge change in processes or procedures, facilitating that change is key. Strategies can be perceived as unsuccessful and create upset about needed changes therefore, change does not occur. When employees had more difficulty with making changes, they reported upset that resulted in errors, reduced product quality, and added re-work. When the process was successfully completed, employees felt at ease. Participants reported feelings of comfort with new processes when they had been able to integrate the new actions into their procedures (Hafner, 2014).

NPOs could face similar difficulties if change lacks proper management. Understanding how organizations and individuals effectively use knowledge they possess can be critical to competency maintenance, sustainability, and market share (Hislop, Bosley, Coombs, & Holland, 2013). NPOs need unlearning techniques to update and retain the important knowledge base they possess. Associates in the knowledge economy, must possess specialized skills to be innovators, create needed skill changes in the fast and flexible environment to meet organizational benchmarks. Additionally, organizations need to strengthen their ability to use knowledge productively to maintain mission, vision, and values into the future. Effective measurement tools in assessment of knowledge and its effect on the organizations and individuals' competitive advantage will benefit as a result.

Conclusion

Competitive advantage not only requires an increase in knowledge but a change in knowledge (Leibowitz, 2000). Technological advances and changes in market conditions increase work pace in environments and require continual updating (Leape & Berwick, 2005). Completing needed organizational goals established by management requires innovation and can yield a competitive advantage (Nissen, 2006). Associates create and use a variety of types of knowledge, change processes become critical. Facilitating knowledge change by avoiding faulty, obsolete knowledge is important to NPOs that are no different in knowledge needs. Understanding of knowledge change processes and the effect on NPO effectiveness, can avoid competency loss.

Unlearning is NPO power to be different during an unstable global environment. Using the skill of thinking differently can help an NPO remain competitive. When an organizational leader selects a method to remove unwanted assumptions and faulty knowledge from the past, they are on their way to unlearning. When there is awareness of a knowledge gap, the time to adapt, and to support those producing the change to organizations to alter trajectory is now. Understanding unlearning can assist in changing mental models, help focus associate training, and assist in the effective updating of processes for NPOs and FPOs alike.

The basic take away lessons are: (a) FPOs and NPOs must be able to adopt changes in order to survive; (b) return to basic strategies that work to facilitate change; and (c) support the personnel that are responsible for making those changes. The remaining question for each associate to ask themselves is, what can I do to replace unproductive, outdated processes, and behaviors that are no longer successful, and impede and limit my future success?

NPO leaders should start by reflecting on current unproductive organizational models and cultural assumptions. Leaders should decide their positioning within the marketplace and what direction they are headed into the future. Assessment and metrics are necessary to creating baseline data to chart a path toward change.

There are six questions for NPO leaders to ask:

1. Whom do you serve?
2. What problem does your NPO solve and how do they solve this problem?
3. How are needs changing and how are you currently solving them?
4. How does your organization facilitate changes?
5. Would an analysis of structure and function provide a new direction and focus?
6. What does your NPO need to unlearn and are you willing to start the conversation?

NPOs need to unlearn. The NPO, built on the premise of solving a societal problem, needs to first look inward to develop and care for associates during times of tumultuous change. Organizational leaders that create a culture of unlearning outdated knowledge will also forge organizational sustainability.

To unlearn the idea that an organization should not maximize profits and reduce costs is not valid and could limit success. When an NPO understands the importance of knowledge as a valuable resource and develops processes to update skills, the organization makes progress. When organizations facilitate and reward successful learning change processes, their ability to compete improves. When NPOs recognize that associates and the knowledge they possess are the organization's most valuable resource, true unlearning of previous mental models can begin.

The implications of maintaining skill competencies during technological advances are clear. NPOs need to remove barriers to unlearning. Making sure that skill competencies are continually updated adds value to the NPO. Innovation through unlearning can develop new ways to think and solve challenges. Maintaining skill competencies on parallel with for-profit sector employees bolsters a NPO's ability to compete effectively by adding this ability to innovate. These fundamental changes ensure that all NPOs are living up to their mission, vision, values, and purpose. Squandering the most valuable resource of individual knowledge cannot continue in this age of knowledge.

Unlearning is a true refractive thinking process. Refractive thinking uses a new lens to develop a new perspective on old thinking. Establishing unlearning of previous NPO mental models develops new capabilities, competencies, and begins to retain associates and their skills. It can be responsible for valuing knowledge, allow for the updating of processes and changing trajectories of organizations. Understanding the unlearning process can improve personal development, can pave the way for all NPOs to grow, keep expenditures in check, and continue to be able to solve long-standing societal problems.

THOUGHTS FROM THE ACADEMIC ENTREPRENEUR

The problem to be solved:

- Changes for both FPOs and NPOs within a knowledge economy creates difficulties in sustainability
- Organizations believe they have unique problems

The goals:

- To understand the importance of knowledge as a valuable resource
- To understand knowledge change, or the unlearning process, to improve organizational response to ever-changing environmental conditions
- To facilitate knowledge change processes to innovate and improve task performance in NPOs and FPOs

The questions to ask:

- Why do NPOs feel that their problems with change are unique?
- How can organizations effectively use unlearning strategies for increased success?
- Can techniques in knowledge change assist NPO associates in successfully developing updated competencies?

Today's Business Application:

- Nonprofit Organizations are not unique.
- Reducing the effects of change using FPO techniques can be key to sustainable success for an NPO.
- Knowledge updating, or modification of competencies can be more difficult than realized
- The knowledge that NPO associates possess is a valuable, often overlooked, resource.

- When an associate is onboard with the mission, vision, and values of an NPO, their knowledge is hard to recapture if they leave.

- Leaders who understand unlearning strategies, know how to effectively manage knowledge for regulatory, technical, societal, and economic changes.

REFERENCES

Akgün, A. E., Byrne, J. C., Lynn, G. S., & Keskin, H. (2007). Organizational unlearning as changes in beliefs and routines in organizations. *Journal of Organizational Change Management, 20*, 794-812. doi:10.1108/09534810710831028

Attewell, P. (1992). Technology diffusion and organizational learning: The case of business computing. *Organizational Science, 3*(1), 1–19. doi:10.1287/orsc.3.1.1

Becker, K. (2011). Individual and organizational unlearning: Directions for future research. *International Journal of Organizational Behavior, 9*, 659- 670. Retrieved from https://eprints.qut.edu.au/10604/1/10604.pdf

Becker, K. (2008). Unlearning as a driver of sustainable change and innovation: Three Australian case studies. *International Journal of Technology Management, 42*(1), 89-106. doi:10.1504/IJTM.2008.018062

Becker, K. L. (2007). *Unlearning in the workplace: A mixed methods* study (Unpublished doctoral dissertation). Queensland University of Technology, Australia. https://eprints.qut.edu.au/16574/

Bloom, B. S., & Krathwohl, D. R. (1956). *Taxonomy of educational objectives: The classification of educational goals* (Handbook 1: Cognitive domain). New York, NY: Longmans. doi:10.1177/001316445601600310

Cegarra-Navarro, J. G., & Dewhurst, F. W. (2006) Linking shared organizational context and relational capital through unlearning: An initial empirical investigation in SMEs. *The Learning Organization, 13*(1), 49–62. doi:10.1108/09696470610639121

Cegarra-Navarro, J. G., & Moya, B. R. (2005). Business performance management and unlearning process. *Knowledge and Process Management, 12*(3), 161-170. doi:10.1002/kpm.233

Cegarra Navarro, J. G., Martinez Martinez, A., Gutiérrez, J., & O. Rodríguez, A. L. L. (2013). Environmental knowledge, unlearning, and performance in hospitality companies. *Management Decision, 51* 341-360. doi:10.1108/00251741311301858

Clark, R. E. (2010). Cognitive and neuroscience research on learning and instruction: Recent insights about the impact of non-conscious knowledge on problem solving, higher order thinking skills and interactive cyber-learning environments. *11th International Conference on Education Research (ICER), New Educational Paradigm for Learning and Instruction,* Seoul, South Korea, 1-24. Retrieved from http://www.aect.org/publications/whitepapers/2010/ICER3.pdf

Griswold, T., & Kaiser, A. (2017). Leaving behind what we are not: Applying a systems thinking perspective to present unlearning as an enabler for finding the best version of the self. *Journal of Organizational Transformation & Social Change,* 14(1), 39-55. doi:10.1080/14779633.2017.1291145

Hafner, J. H., Ellis, T. J., & Hafner, W. (2014, January). Error occurrence: Successful versus unsuccessful unlearning in individuals. In System Sciences (HICSS), 2014 47th Hawaii International Conference on (pp. 3509-3514). Institute of Electrical and Electronics Engineers (IEEE). doi:10.1109/HICSS.2014.437

Hafner, J. H. (2014). *A conceptualization of unlearning in organizational employees* (Doctoral dissertation). Retrieved from ProQuest Dissertations and Theses database. (UMI No. 3639829)

Hafner, J. H. (2015). Computer system unlearning in individuals. (2015). 48th Hawaii International Conference on System Science. In *2015 48th Hawaii International Conference on System Science (HICSS). January 05-08, 2015.* doi:10.1109/HICSS.2015.463

Hafner, J. H., & Noteboom, C. (2015a). Challenges of change: Technological ease or technological upset? *21st Americas Conference on Information Systems (AMCIS 2015).* 13-15 August 2015, Fajardo, Puerto Rico. Available at https://www.researchgate.net/publication/283083616_Challenges_of_change_technological_ease_or_technological_upset

Hafner, J. H., & Noteboom, C. B. (2015b). Does unlearning impact interaction of EHR end-users? *ICHITA,* 50. Retrieved from https://scholarworks.wmich.edu/ichita_transactions/55

Hafner, J. H. (2016). Does incomplete unlearning impact medical errors? (2016). *49th Hawaii International Conference on System Sciences (HICSS). 5-8 Jan. 2016 Koloa, HI* (pp. 4324-4333). Institute of Electrical and Electronics Engineers (IEEE). doi:10.1109/HICSS.2016.537

Hedberg, B. (1981). How organizations learn and unlearn. In P. Nystrom & W. H. Starbuck (Eds.), *Handbook of organizational design* (Vol. 1, pp. 1-26). London, England: Cambridge University Press.

Hislop, D., Bosley, S., Coombs, C. R., &and Holland, J. (2013). The process of individual unlearning: A neglected topic in an under-researched field. *Management Learning, 45,* 540–560. doi:10.1177/1350507613486423

Kessler, G. (2011). What business can learn from the nonprofit (and vice versa): Drucker revisited An Interview with Tim Shriver, CEO, Special Olympics, *People* and Strategy, 34(3), 40-44. Retrieved from: http://kateskesler.com/wp-content/uploads/2012/08/Shriver_Interview

King, D. (2016). Becoming business-like: Governing the nonprofit professional. *Nonprofit and Voluntary Sector Quarterly, 46*(2), 241-260. https://dx.doi.org/10.1177/0899764016663321

Kong, E., & Farrell, M. (2010). Knowledge and learning capabilities in nonprofit organizations: A relational capital perspective. *The International Journal of Learning, 17*(3), 97-116. Retrieved from: https://eprints.usq.edu.au/8639/1/Kong_Farrell_IJL_v17n3_PV.pdf

Leibowitz, J. (2000). *Building organizational intelligence: A knowledge management primer.* Boca Raton, FL: CRC Press.

Leibowitz, J., & Beckman, T. (1998). *Knowledge organizations: What every manager should know.* Boca Raton, FL: CRC Press.

Leape, L. L., & Berwick, D. M. (2005). Five years after to err is human what have we learned? *Journal of the American Medical Association, 29,* 2384-2390. doi:10.1001/jama.293.19.2384

Low, P. K. C. (2011). Must we unlearn to learn? *International Research Journals, 2,* 1801-1809. Retrieved from hhtp://www.interesjournals.org/ER

Newstrom, J. W. (1983). The management of unlearning: Exploding the *"Clean Slate"* fallacy. *Training and Development Journal, 37*(8), 36-39. Retrieved from https://eric.ed.gov/?id=EJ306251

Nissen, M. E. (2006). *Harnessing knowledge dynamics: principled organizational knowing & learning,* Hershey, PA: IRM Press.

Nystrom, P. C., & Starbuck, W. H. (1984). To avoid organizational crisis, unlearn. *Organizational Dynamics, 12*(4), 53-65. doi:10.1016/0090-2616(84)90011-1

Noteboom, C. B., Hafner, J., & Wahbeh, A. (2017). Characteristics of complete and incomplete physicians' unlearning with electronic medical record. *Journal of the Midwest Association for Information Systems, 2017*(2), 57. Retrieved from https://aisel.aisnet.org/jmwais/vol2017/iss2/5

Nystrom, P. C., & Starbuck, W. H. (1984). To avoid organizational crisis, unlearn. *Organizational Dynamics, 12*(4), 53-65. doi:10.1016/0090-2616(84)90011-1

McInerney, C. R., & Day, R. E. (2007). *Rethinking knowledge management* (Vol. 12). Berlin, Germany: Springer-Verlag.

Miller, R. H., West, C., Brown, T. M., Sim, I., & Ganchoff, C. (2005). The value of electronic health records in solo or small group practices: Physicians' EHR adoption is slowed by a reimbursement system that rewards the volume of services more than it does their quality. *Health Affairs,* 1127–1137. doi:10.1377/hlthaff.24.5.1127

Neal, D. T., Wood, W., Labreque, J. S., & Lally, P. (2012). How do habits guide behavior? Perceived and actual triggers of habits in daily life. *Journal of Experimental Social Psychology, 48,* 492-498. doi:10.1016/j.jesp.2011.10.011

Nonaka, I., & von Krogh, G. (2009). Tacit knowledge and knowledge conversion: Controversy and advancement in organizational knowledge creation theory. *Organization Science, 20,* 635–652. doi:10.1287/orsc.1080.0412

Ouellette, J. A., & Wood, W. (1998). Habit and intention in everyday life: The multiple processes by which past behavior predicts future behavior. *Psychological Bulletin,* 124(1), 54-74. doi:10.1037/0033-2909.124.1.54

Rushmer, R., & Davies, H. T. (2004). Unlearning in health care. *Quality and Safety in Health Care,* 13(suppl II), ii, 10-15. doi:10.1136/qsch.2003.009506

Shaffer, L. (2017, June 23). Why 'unlearning' old habits is an essential step for innovation, *Mindshift.* Retrieved from https://www.kqed.org/mindshift/48480/why-unlearning-old-habits-is-an-essential-step-for-innovation

Schmorrow, D., Cohn, J., & Nicholson, D. (Eds.). (2009). *The PSI handbook of virtual environments for training and education: Developments for the military and beyond* (Vol. 1). Westport, CT: Praeger Security International. doi:10.5860/choice.46-6247

Senge, P. M. (2006). *The fifth discipline: The art and practice of the learning organization.* New York, NY: Doubleday.

Starbuck, W. H. (1996). Unlearning ineffective or obsolete technologies. Information Systems Working Papers Series. *International Journal of Technology Management,* 11, 725. doi:10.1504/IJTM.1996.025463

Starkey, K., Tempest, S., & McKinlay, A. (2004). *How organizations learn: Managing the search for knowledge* (2nd ed.). London, UK: Thompson Learning.

Topaloglu, O., McDonald, R. E., & Hunt, S. D., (2018) The theoretical foundations of nonprofit competition: a resource-advantage theory approach, *Journal of Nonprofit & Public Sector Marketing,* 30(3), 229-250. doi:10.1080/10495142.2018.1452818 Topaloglu

Tsang, E. W. K., & Zahra, S. A. (2008). Organizational unlearning. *Human Relations,* 16, 1435-1462. doi:10.1177/0018726708095710

Wheatley M. (2006). Leadership lessons for the real world. *Leader to Leader, 41,* 16-20. doi:10.1002/ltl.185

Wood, W., & Neal, D. T. (2016). Habit-based behavior change interventions. Los Angeles, CA: Department of Psychology. University of Southern California Catalyst Behavioral Sciences. https://dx.doi.org/10.1353/bsp.2016.0008

Wood, W., Tam, L., & Witt, M. G. (2005). Changing circumstances, disrupting habits. *Journal of Personality and Social Science,* 918-933. doi:10.1037/0022-3514.88.6.918

About the Author . . .

Julee H. Hafner, M.S.CCC-SLP, Ph.D. resides in the historic town of Melbourne, Florida. Dr. Julee, is a Communication Strategist who partners with executives and solopreneurs to grow their professional brands, human-to-human. Communicating effectively with all types of people is an essential skill, no matter what the industry. Dr. Julee, an expert speaker, whose audiences have fun learning how to communicate with style, unleashing the power of communication, engage employees, and drive performance.

Dr. Julee holds a Ph.D. in Leadership from The Chicago School of Professional Psychology, a M.S. in Communication from Towson University, and a B.A. in English from the University of Pittsburgh. She is a John Maxwell certified speaker and coach, D.I.S.C. certified, and a President's Club member of Sandler Sales Training.

Dr. Julee received The Graduate Research Award from TCS, serves as a dissertation coach and Chair for 2 minitracks at the Hawaiian International Conference on System Science (HICSS), presented papers at HICSS, AMCIS, and ICHITA, Editor for International Journal of Knowledge Management (IJKM) and other journal publications.

She is an author of more than six academic publications. Additional published works include her dissertation: *Unlearning in Organizational Employees*, academic papers, and two books: *The 7 Tactics to Communication Completions* and *The 7 Tactics to Communication Completions: The Workbook*.

To reach Dr. Julee Hafner for information on speaking, or professional coaching, please visit her **website:** https://www.drjuleehafner.com/ or **e-mail**: drjuleehafner@gmail.com

CHAPTER 3

Financial Distress at Nonprofit Organizations

Dr. Frank Musmar

People understand the term *nonprofit* or *not-for-profit* as organizations that did not make a profit. However, nonprofits and not-for-profits reinvest their margin within the organization to stay operative and support the organizational goals. The organizational structure of nonprofit is similar to for-profit organizations; however, nonprofit is tax exempt because they do not pay dividends to stockholders and they reinvest their profit to support the organizational mission. Examples of nonprofit organizations are the American Red Cross and the American Heart Association. In this chapter of The Refractive Thinker®, I present an overview of the status of financial stability and organizational performance in the nonprofit organizations

Executive directors of nonprofit organizations have mounting financial pressures to survive in a constrained budgetary environment. Nonprofit organizations closed at 30% rates exceeding those for-profit organizations (Needleman & Ko, 2012). U. S. nonprofit organizations are local institutions that play a social role in improving education, alleviating poverty, providing economic opportunities, and supporting the health care system, which accounts for a sizable portion of public sector budgets (Richards, 2014). Executive directors need to implement effective strategies to improve organizational performance. Using a refractive thinking approach, executive directors might gain new insight that they can use to improve organizational performance of their organizations.

Background: History and Importance of Avoiding Financial Distress

The number of nonprofit organizations in financial crises that can lead to insolvency and closure in the United States increased from 2014 through 2017 (Chuang, Liu, Lu, & Lee, 2014; Kelley et al., 2012). Thirty percent of nonprofit organizations had negative 3 year net income margins from 2014 through 2017 (GUIDSTAR, 2018). The consequences of financial distress lead to insolvency and potential liquidity (Rosenberg & Ferlie, 2014). The disastrous consequences of financial distress includes discontinuity of operations, administrative expenses, and legal costs (Carlson et al., 2014). Mazumder and Miller (2014) indicated the necessity to assess the financial conditions of the firm in a regular base to evaluate it's liquidity position. Predicting business failure will help management take preventive measures, such as operational policy changes, reorganizing the firm's financial structure, voluntary liquidation, and adopting sound corporate governance practices (Mazumder & Miller, 2014). The purpose of this study was to explore the strategies that nonprofit executive directors use to improve organizational performance to prevent financial distress.

Financial Distress

Nonprofit organizations financial distress is a common problem in the United States. Thirty percent of nonprofit organizations were financially distressed based on a negative total profit margin from 2014 to 2017 (Richards, 2014). Very few authors to date assessed in studies the effect of financial distress on quality of service indicators. Despite the limited research on this topic, Richards (2014) suggested a significant relationship exists between financial distress and service outcomes.

Xu, Xiao, Dang, Yang, and Yang (2014) studied the relationship between financial distress, organizational performance, and corporate governance. Using companies listed on the Taiwan Stock Exchange, Xu et al. found that the ability of smaller organizations to recover from financial distress depends on it's corporate governance practices. The researchers also stated that financial and corporate governance variables could better predict financial distress rather than macroeconomic variables (Xu, Xiao, Dang, Yang, & Yang, 2014).

Bunyaminu and Bashiru (2014) mentioned that most of the failed organizations showed signs of financial distress long before the failures occurred. The methodologies and models for predicting business failure include univariate and multivariate analysis (Bunyaminu & Bashiru, 2014). Univariate models include the use of financial ratios such as liquidity and coverage ratios to predict financial distress. However, financial ratios are ineffective because financial ratios are unique to specified industries and provide information only in the context of comparison. After reviewing the literature, few researchers assessed the relationship between financial distress and service outcomes. The refractive thinking in this chapter uses the limited amount of evidence existed regarding the validity of various measures of nonprofit organizations financial distress to improve organizational performance.

Corporate Financial Distress

Lin, Yu, and Zhang (2014) determined financial distress regarding solvency by developing a theoretical model of corporate risk management in the presence of financial distress. The model considered costs associated with financial distress as an intermediate state between solvency and insolvency. When a company misses interest payments or violates debt covenants, distress occurs. The transformation from a solvent to an insolvent state occurs on the date of maturity if the terminal value of the company's assets is lower than the face value of debt. This definition clearly distinguishes financial distress from default and possible bankruptcy. A company can be distressed without defaulting. However, default and bankruptcy are not possible without the preceding period of financial distress (Lin, Yu, and Zhang, 2014). In their study, Bazzoli, Fareed, and Waters (2014) showed that financial distress has different financial characteristics than bankruptcy. The features of financial distress are cumulative negative earnings over at least a few consecutive years, losses, and poor performance. And the conclusion to draw is determining financial distress at an early stages might save the organization from default.

Organizations in financial distress have the choice to restructure its debt and reach an appropriate level of solvency. The company can merge and disappear as an independent business entity or file for bankruptcy as a strategic response by the management or owners to financial problems. Jhass (2013) and Bunyaminu and Bashiru (2014) stressed a legal and strategic character of bankruptcy. Bunyaminu and Bashiru criticized the identification of financial distress with bankruptcy procedure because strategic filing for Chapter 11 can happen even if a company is economically solvent. Filing for Chapter 11 is especially suspicious without going through financial distress beforehand. Reexamining the predictive ability of auditor's opinions regarding corporate bankruptcy, Jhass (2013) confirmed this hypothesis and noted that management fraud derives bankruptcy without preceding financial distress rather than by a naturally stressed situation. The concept of financial distress seems to have a significant distinction from the theory of bankruptcy. Unlike filing for Chapter 11, financial distress does not depend on the legal procedure of a single country; instead, financial distress is an initial period of the distress cycle, allowing the company to reflect, react, and recover without having to bear the administrative and direct costs of bankruptcy procedures.

Edmonstone (2013) identified financial distress when a business experiences losses over at least 3 consecutive years. Results of empirical analysis of the dividend policy in financial distress indicated that after a company enters into financial distress, the company usually experiences cash flow problems and is unable to pay dividends (Edmonstone, 2013). Therefore, rapid and aggressive dividend reductions together with consecutive negative income are an alarming signal of a financial distress situation.

Different approaches to the definition of the term *financial distress* indicated how this economic category is versatile, sophisticated, and sometimes controversial. The refractive thinking in the theory of financial distress is to interpret as dependent on the purpose of research under a particular point of view, financial, operational, or legal circumstances. Interpreting the financial distress circumstances will lead to using this term interchangeably with other similar financial definitions.

Risk Factors Contributing to Financial Distress

Adams, Muir, and Hoque (2014) divided all possible causes of financial distress into two groups: internal risk factors and external shocks. Internal risk factors are an attribution to poor management. Potential forms of the appearance of bad management are the absence of a sense of a need for change, inadequate communication, overexpansion, unintentionally improper handling of projects, or fraud. External shocks are independent of managerial skills (Adams et al., 2014). External shocks are inefficiencies in regulatory development, turbulence in the labor market, or natural disasters.

Similar to Adams et al. (2014) but providing additional detail in distinguishing between external and internal risk factors, Kash, Spaulding, Gamm, and Johnson (2013) examined the proportion of every risk factor within each group. Kash et al. revealed five significant sources of external risk: economic change, competitive change, government constraints, social alterations, and technological change.

The review of the literature indicated that while in the 1990s the internal risk factors derived financial distress, in the 2000s researchers reported an upward of external sources of financial distress. Adams et al. (2014) offered a possible explanation for this trend: the evolutionary development of corporate enterprises, the change to service-oriented economies and the increase of the governmental regulation, provoke a shift from internal to external causes of corporate failure. Financial distress occurs because of management's failing ability to control and anticipate negative economic effects on the firm's profitability and future prosperity. In the sample by Adams et al., unanticipated economic shocks cause about 15% to 40% of all distressed situations.

Financial distress can have a detrimental influence on the performance of non-profit organizations. Kim and Partington (2014) stated that nonprofit organizations management should monitor potential financial distress efficiently and predict a response depending on the severity of the circumstances. The researchers examined multiple factors that might explain the financial distress of nonprofit hospitals during 1998 to 2001 and indicated a connection between the decrease in (a) occupancy rates, (b) the increase in Medicaid payer mix, (c) health maintenance organization penetration, (d) market competition, (e) physician supply, and (f) the financial distress of urban hospitals.

The summary of the risk factors contributing to financial distress since 1998 falls into two groups: external risk factors versus internal risk factors. The most prominent internal sources of financial distress are bad management, poor operational performance, and high advantage. External reasons for financial distress are economic shocks, overcapacity and structural changes, deregulation of the key industries as well as natural disasters. Sometimes researchers take a wrong path by oversimplifying the real reasons for financial trouble. However the refractive thinking is to draw a line between the two groups of factors. When managerial incompetence represents the most frequent causal factor of entry into financial distress, the reasons in many cases are mixed, interrelated, and should be analyzed in all complexity.

Dimensions of Financial Distress

The dynamic nature of financial distress varies according to the separate stages and attributes of each stage of distress; the company passes through separate stages, each of which has specific attributes and consequently, contributes differently to corporate failure (Trotta, Cardamone, Cavallaro, & Mauro, 2013). Changes in financial attributes affect the transition from one state of financial distress to another. When financial attributes become aggravated, the company will face bankruptcy; if the financial performance improves, the business has a chance to overcome its financial difficulties and recover without defaulting. Analysis of the corporate failure should exploit three main dimensions: behavior over the period, the effect on different financial states, and the performance at various distress stages (Virtue, Chaussale, & Kelly, 2013).

The behavior over the period covers the period from the first signs of slight deterioration in performance through accelerated impairment down to the deepest point and subsequent recovery. Financial distress cycle is the behavior over the period (Fuxiu, Bing, & Jicheng, 2013). Determination of the average length of the failure process does not apply because of difficulties in the measurement of the onset of financial distress. Ex-ante predictions cannot estimate the date when bankruptcy occurs by more than 3 years in advance (Saxby, 2013). Predicting default more than 3 years before bankruptcy significantly reduces the accuracy of the forecasting models. An ex-post analysis of financial distress shows that the first observable signs of the deterioration of corporate health appear five to six years before bankruptcy (Parry, Mumford, Bower, & Watts, 2014). The existence of earlier signs of declining performance is unobservable, fragile, mostly of strategic and not of a financial nature, and therefore, difficult to measure. Financial managers usually ignore these factors because of low significance. Adverse developments become observable about 1 to 2 years before default when the company becomes severely distressed. Recovery takes 2-3 years after default to restructure the debt of the company and achieve a predistressed level of performance (Spruit, Vroon, & Batenburg, 2014).

The financial state of the organization represents the second dimension of the corporate failure process. The fall of business into distress usually happens because of a shift in liquidity. However, a reduction of liquid resources does not necessarily have an adverse influence on a firm's solvency position (Trotta et al., 2013). Typically, in the early stages of financial distress, the company continues to be solvent, which makes it difficult to recognize the existence of negative processes in the enterprise. Deepening financial distress triggers the illiquidity of the firm's assets; the value of the firm deteriorates below some lower threshold. In this case, the financial state of the company is not stable anymore (Fuxiu et al., 2013). Financial distress does not necessarily lead to default, in this period the company remains solvent this implies that it is possible that the financial position will improve before the date of maturity of the debt (Bazzoli, Fareed, & Waters, 2014).

The distressed but solvent state has different characteristics than the solvent state. The acceleration falls in value emphasizing an increasing role of the advantage in the detection of a possible transformation to insolvency. Change in financial status to the insolvent state happens on the date of maturity when the company defaults on repaying its debt. The legal consequence of this event is bankruptcy. Transformation or the return to the solvent state is only possible after successful completion of distressed debt restructuring (Jhass, 2013).

Effective Strategies to Improve Organizational Performance

Executive directors of the nonprofit organizations use several strategies to prevent financial distress and improve organizational performance. To get an understanding of current strategies nonprofit organizations executive directors use to improve organizational performance, I interviewed 10 participants with experience implementing effective organizational performance strategies. Below, is the discussion of some of the strategies participants found to be useful to reduce financial distress including effective leadership, skills development, continuous learning, and customer focus strategy. In the findings below, P stands for participant, and the number following the P represents the order of interviewed participants. For example, the first participant is P1. The data analysis from the interview revealed that refractive thinkers and leaders who can effectively implement a successful performance strategy could help their organizations achieve its mission by effective leadership, improving organization performance, and promoting continuous learning.

Effective Leadership Improved Organizational Performance

Effective leadership that improved organizational performance was the first theme that emerged from exploring the participants' responses. The participants articulated that effective leadership is important to strategy development and improving the organization's financial performance. P1 stated, "Effective leadership improved the performance of the organization." P4 expressed,

"Particular leaders use their effective leadership skills and organizational assessments to ensure that the organization's performance levels are stable." P2 said that effective leadership provides a successful environment for improving organizational performance. P5 noted that the organization's financial performance increased after the leadership started managing properly. Some participants stated that of the many effective leadership skills, effective communication is one of the essential strategic leadership skills that contribute to improving the organization's performance (P1, P4, P7, P8, P9, and P10). P1 revealed that effective communication leadership leads to superior performance within an organization. The rest of the participants articulated that effective leadership is important to strategy development and improving the organization's financial performance (P6, P7, P8, P9, and P10). Effective leadership skills such as effective communication skills improved the organizational performance was consistent with the findings of Kim and Partington (2014), who also found that effective communication leadership led to the superior performance of an organization and concluded that effective leadership is essential to both strategy development and organizational performance (Kim & Partington, 2014).

According to some participants, a leadership commitment is an effective strategic leadership skill that contributed to the organization's performance (P2, P3, P5, and P6). When asked about the positive outcomes from using the identified strategies for improving organizational performance, some participants mentioned that a committed management team with effective leadership skills sets the direction and evaluates the performance of the organization (P1, P3, P5, P6, and P9). Highlighting leadership commitment as an effective strategic leadership skill is consistent with the findings of Meena and Thakkar (2014). The authors found that the leadership commitments improved the leadership skills and the performance of the leader (Meena & Thakkar, 2014). Specifically,

P1 through P10 mentioned that creation, inspiration, and effective communication are essential leadership skills that senior management and directors must exhibit to enhance the health care business performance. These findings remain consistent with the findings of Richards (2014), who concluded that effective leadership is essential to both strategy development and performance.

While the participants at the health care center deliberated about the positive outcomes of effective leadership skills, they considered the negative outcomes of poor leadership as well. P7 stated, "Poor leadership has several negative outcomes. Poor leadership affects the way the business makes money; shareholders lose their funds, and employees lose their jobs." Additionally, P6 revealed that an organization that has corporate leaders who are reckless would fail the organization. Another participant (P3) indicated that ineffective leaders affect the financial performance of the health care business; they can fail or promote the organization at their end. Concurring with this notion, P4 emphasized that ineffective leaders can influence the organization's performance in a negative way when there is an issue of personal interest. P1 indicated that poor leadership might be the result of a leader's conflict of interest that has the potential to affect a business performance negatively. The findings that poor leadership negatively affects business performance are consistent with the findings of Tarigan and Widjaja (2014) who also found that leaders and board of directors need effective decision-making skills to make safe decisions that contribute effectively to the strategic plan of the organization.

The participants talked about the attributes of successful leaders on business performance. P1 noted that in situations when corporate leaders are honest, transparent, and professional in dealing with the institution they manage, the business is often successful. P7 stated that professional and transparent leaders set the example by aligning actions with integrity and values and by creating a spirit of community, which increases the communication levels within the organization, and improves the overall performance. Participants indicated that integrity, honesty, and leading by example are the most successful attributes of successful leadership (P2, P3, P4, P6, and P9). P5 noted that integrity is an attribute of successful leaders. Adams, Muir, and Hoque (2014) addressed the attributes of successful leaders in business performance. The authors found that the appearance of weak performance attributed to bad management, the absence of a sense of a need for change, inadequate communication, overexpansion, unintentionally improper handling of projects, and fraud (Adams et al., 2014). Theme 1 relates to Robert Kaplan and David Norton's (1992) BSC. Mazumder and Miller (2014) communicated that organization's performance depends on the leadership performance. Effective leaders work in the best interest of the business to maximize the investors' wealth (Mazumder & Miller, 2014). In the context of the Musmar (2017) study, poor leadership impedes performance.

Training, Skills Development, and Continuous Learning Improved Performance

Training, skills development, and continuous learning improved performance were part of the second theme that emerged from exploring the participants' responses. P1 stated, "Continuous learning increased some of my co-worker's productivity and performance." P4 mentioned that because of the constant training activities that leadership implemented, employees' job skills improved, as well as their overall job performance. Along those lines, P3 stated, "In general, the health care organization leadership used continuous learning programs as an instrument to increase employee productivity and motivation." Mentioning continuous learning, P10 noted, "The continuous learning programs implemented reinforce the organization's leadership core values of commitment, improvement, quality, pride, and integrity. I am grateful to gain new knowledge and skills while improving my performance."

On the same topic, P7 stated, "Continuous learning helped our personnel to update their skills, remain marketable in the workplace, and improve their overall performance." Some participants expressed that the continuous learning process is essential because it enabled employees to develop and refine their skills to increase productivity for the organization's day-to-day operations (P2, P5, P6, and P9). The findings related to continuous learning programs that improve employee's performance are consistent with the findings of Rosenberg and Ferlie (2014) who also found that continuous learning leads to business performance success. Rosenberg and Ferlie noted that by implementing new procedures and improving employee skills, continuous learning and growth might enhance firm value, investment performance, and productivity.

The participants articulated how continuous training and learning is important to improve organizational performance. Four participants articulated that the continuous training and skills development programs implemented by the health care organization leadership did not merely improve the employee performance, but the programs enabled management to improve the organization's business performance (P3, P5, P7, and P9). P8 stated, "Leadership implemented a key component of the continuous learning system with a variety of learning methods, including classroom training, mentoring, and participation in workshops to improve organizational performance." P2 mentioned that involving personnel in constant training activities improved employees' skills to handle job responsibilities. Subsequently, employees focused on accomplishing objectives while increasing the organization's business performance using skills learned from training. According to P1, "The productivity and motivation of our employees are essential to improving organizational performance and providing quality services to the community we serve." P4 noted that a proactive approach to employee skills development is essential to business success to maximize performance. To improve the organizational performance, leadership started engaging employees in organizational strategies, applying lifelong training programs that helped in improving the organization's overall performance (P1 through P10).

Krishnan, Ravindran, and Joshi (2014) found that incorporating the learning and growth perspective in the performance measurement, through employee engagement, training, and healthy corporate culture yields both individual as well as corporate performance improvements. Furthermore, Krishnan et al. (2014) concluded that when trained, employees' skills might improve organizational performance and productivity could increase. Theme 2 relates to Kaplan and Norton's (1992) balanced scorecard model theory. Meena and Thakkar (2014) communicated that the learning and growth perspective of the BSC aligns closely to employees and organizational performance; specifically, continuous training and skills development improve or impede performance. In the context of the Musmar (2017) study, continuous training and skills development improved performance. The managers who implemented continuous learning programs ensured better performances of the employees and the organization (Meena & Thakkar, 2014).

When asked what the most effective strategies for improving organizational performance were, P1 indicated:

> I start working for this company in 2010, and the organization's performance and financial standings were low for 5 years because of lowering the productivity expectations. It was to the point that the board members were ready to close the business because some of the members felt that a weak performance would lead to losing not just employees but also the business. However, since 2015 our performance levels have improved because implementing continuous training programs and score matrix programs.

Customer Focus Strategy Increased Customer Satisfaction

Customer focus strategy increased customer satisfaction was the third theme that emerged. At the health care center, P1 stated, "The outcomes of implementing a customer-focused strategy are; building long-term revenue by winning customer trust, attracting new customers, and maximizing operational performance." P8 stated, "Embedding a proven customer focus strategy might create long-term customer retention and long-term revenue. Every business might have unhappy customers; companies with the best customer service could still lose some of their customers to competitors." Continuing with that theme, P5 mentioned that using a customer focus strategy might increase customer satisfaction and retention, which might increase a company's profitability. Training our employees to apply the principles of a customer focus strategy is our top priority to improve organizational performance." Six of the participants articulated that using a customer focus strategy to measure customer satisfaction might reduce the number of unhappy customers (P3, P4, P5, P7, P9, and P10). Monitoring and improving patient-focus care led to improvements in the levels of customer satisfaction and financial profitability and concluded that there is a significant relationship between hospital financial performance and patient satisfaction (Emami & Doolen, 2015).

The participants articulated how customer satisfaction is important to improve organizational performance. P10 stated, "Customers are looking for maximum satisfaction when spending their money. Some customers complain when they receive bad service, and some don't waste time complaining because they take their business elsewhere." P9 mentioned, "Customer satisfaction, sales performance, and customer retention rates are performance indicators for effective strategies." Along those lines, P7 stated, "When customer satisfaction rates drop below 60%, it is a serious indication of a weak performance." P5 revealed that the main indicator of customer dissatisfaction is a poor customer retention rate over consecutive years. Continuing with that theme, P2 said, "Customers make their buying decisions based on their level of satisfaction and service perceptions, not by my perception. Improving the knowledge of customer satisfaction and buying decisions could improve the organization's business performance." The findings that customer satisfaction is important to improve the organizational performance are similar to the findings of Verbano and Crema (2013) who also found that customer satisfaction led to the superior performance of an organization and concluded that the three critical prominent performance indicators are customer satisfaction, sales performance, and customer retention rate.

Theme 3 relates to Kaplan and Norton's (1992) balanced scorecard model theory. Meena and Thakkar (2014) communicated that the customer perspective of the BSC aligns closely to customer focus strategy. Leaders incorporate the customer satisfaction in the performance measurement by utilizing a customer focus strategy to improve corporate performance and enhance the organization financial stability (Meena & Thakkar, 2014). In the context of the Musmar (2017) study, utilizing customer focus strategy increased customer satisfaction rate and enhanced the organization financial stability.

Conclusion

Nonprofit organizations executive directors can detect financial distress and improve organizational performance by using an effective leadership style, skills development, continuous learning and customer focus strategy. The strategies shared by participants might help executive directors promote organizational commitment, increase productivity, and improve the organization financial stability. Nonprofit organizations executive directors need to consider and implement the above strategies as a way to improve organizational performance in their organizations. Implementing these strategies is less expensive than the costs associated with financial distress. Therefore, recommendations include that nonprofit organizations executive directors, scholars, and practitioners use the findings and recommendations of this study to gain new insight into financial distress reduction strategies shared by experienced professionals. Nonprofit organizations executive directors who can use a refractive thinking approach in the implementation of effective organizational performance strategies might bring long-term success to their organizations.

THOUGHTS FROM THE ACADEMIC ENTREPRENEUR

The problem to be solved:

- Reducing financial distress in the non-profit organizations
- Improving organizations' performance by applying the required strategies

The goals:

- Exploring the strategies that non-profit organizations Executive Directors use to prevent financial distress
- Improving organizational performance for sustainability

The questions to ask:

- What strategies do you use to prevent financial distress and improve organizational performance for sustainability?
- What strategies were most effective in improving organizational performance?
- What are a few positive outcomes from using the identified strategies for improving organizational performance?
- What assessments do you use to assess financial risk and organizational performance?

Today's Business Application:

- Effective leaders, who understand performance management can increase productivity and profitability, promote organizational commitment, which leads to organizational growth.
- The future of non-profit organizations depends on leaders' ability to retain top performers.
- Supportive leaders can increase organizational productivity and performance, which in turn promotes increased sustainability.

REFERENCES

Adams, C. A., Muir, S., & Hoque, Z. (2014). Measurement of sustainability performance in the public sector. *Sustainability Accounting, Management and Policy Journal, 5*(1), 46-67. doi:10.1108/sampj-04-2012-0018

Bazzoli, G. J., Fareed, N., & Waters, T. M. (2014). Hospital financial performance in the recent recession and implications for institutions that remains financially weak. *Health Affairs, 33,* 739-745. doi:10.1377/hlthaff.2013.0988

Bazzoli, G. J., Lee, W., Hsieh, H. M., & Mobley, L. R. (2012). The effects of safety net hospital closures and conversions on patient travel distance to hospital services. *Health Services Research, 47*(1), 129-150. doi:10.1111/j.1475-6773.2011.01318.x

Beck, C. D. (2014). Antecedents of servant leadership: A mixed methods study. *Journal of Leadership & Organizational Studies, 21*(3), 299-314. doi:10.1177/1548051814529993

Bristol, S. T., & Hicks, R. W. (2014). Protecting boundaries of consent in clinical research implications for improvement. *Nursing Ethics, 21*(1), 16-27. doi:10.1177/0969733013487190

Bryde, D., Broquetas, M., & Volm, J. M. (2013). The project benefits of building information modeling (BIM). *International Journal of Project Management, 31,* 971-980. doi:10.1016/j.ijproman.2012.12.001

Carlson, M., Lewis, K., & Nelson, W. (2014). Using policy intervention to identify financial stress. *International Journal of Finance & Economics, 19*(1), 59-72. doi:10.1002/ijfe.1482

Chuang, T. C., Liu, J. S., Lu, L. Y. Y., & Lee, Y. (2014). The main paths of medical tourism: From transplantation to beautification. *Tourism Management, 45,* 49-58. doi:10.1016/j.tourman.2014.03.016

Darvish, H., Mohammadi, M., & Afsharpour, P. (2012). Studying the knowledge management effect of promoting the four balanced scorecard perspectives: A case study at SAIPA automobile manufacturing. *Word & Text: Journal of Literary Studies & Linguistics, 1,* 9-23. Retrieved from http://jlsl.upg-ploiesti.ro

Draper, A., & Swift, J. A. (2011). Qualitative research in nutrition and dietetics: Data collection issues. *Journal of Human Nutrition & Dietetics, 24,* 3-12. doi:10.1111/j.1365-277X.2010.01117.x

ElBannan, M. A., & ElBannan, M. A. (2014). Corporate governance and accounting performance: A balanced scorecard approach. *Accounting and Finance Research, 3*(2), 60-77. doi:10.5430/afr.v3n2p60

Emami, A., & Doolen, T. (2015). Healthcare performance measurement: Identification of metrics for the learning and growth balanced scorecard perspective. *International Journal of Industrial Engineering, 22,* 426-437. Retrieved from http://journals.sfu.ca/ijietap/index.php/ijie/article/view/1221

Erbasi, A. (2014). Use of Balanced Scorecard in municipality performance assessments: Municipal scorecard model. *Journal of Advanced Management Science, 2*(3), 197-205. doi:10.12720/joams.2.3.197-205

Fuxiu J., Bing Z., & Jicheng H., (2013). CEO's financial experience and earnings management. *Journal of Multinational Financial Management, 23*(3), 134-145. doi:10.1016/j.mulfin.2013.03.005

Grigoroudis, E., Orfanoudaki, E., & Zopounidis, C. (2012). Strategic performance measurement in a healthcare organisation: A multiple criteria approach based on balanced scorecard. *Omega, 40*(1), 104-119. doi:10.1016/j.omega.2011.04.001

Harper, M., & Cole, P. (2012). Member checking: Can benefits be gained similar to group therapy? *The Qualitative Report, 17,* 510-517. Retrieved from http://www.nova.edu

Jhass, P. (2013). Improving outcomes in infected wounds. *British Journal of Healthcare Management, 19,* 429-433. doi:10.12968/bjhc.2013.19.9.429

Kim, M. H., & Partington, G. (2014). Dynamic forecasts of financial distress of Australian firms. *Australian Journal of Management, 40*(1), 135-160. doi:10.1177/0312896213514237

Ko, M., Needleman, J., Derose, K. P., Laugesen, M. J., & Ponce, N. A. (2014). Residential segregation and the survival of U.S. urban public hospitals. *Medical Care Research and Review, 71*(3), 243-260. doi:10.1177/1077558713515079

Krishnan, A., Ravindran, R., & Joshi, P. L. (2014). Performance measurement link between the balanced scorecard dimensions: An empirical study of the manufacturing sector in Malaysia. *AAJFA, 4,* 426-442. doi:10.1504/aajfa.2014.067016

Kordnaeij, A., Salmasi, M., & Fruzande, S. (2011). Evaluation of strategies implementation with BSC approach in Iranian insurance firms. *European Journal of Scientific, 57*(2), 265-274. Retrieved from http://www.europeanjournalofscientificresearch.com

Lech, A. (2013). Corporate social responsibility and financial performance. Theoretical and empirical aspects. *Comparative Economic Research, 16*(3). doi:10.2478/cer-2013-0018

Lupi, S., Verzola, A., Carandina, G., Salani, M., Antonioli, P., & Gregorio, P. (2011). Multidimensional evaluation of performance with experimental application of balanced scorecard: A two year experience. *Cost Effectiveness and Resource Allocation: C / E, 1,* 7. doi:10.1186/1478-7547-9-7.

Manoni, R., Mushi, D., Kessy, J., Salome, S., & Naja, B. (2014). Does training on performance-based financing make a difference in performance and quality of health care delivery? Health care provider's perspective in Rungwe Tanzania. *BMC Health Services Research, 14*(1), 154. doi:10.1186/1472-6963-14-154

Mazumder, B., & Miller, S. (2014). *The effects of the Massachusetts health reform on financial distress* No. 2014-01). Working Paper, Federal Reserve Bank of Chicago. doi:10.2139/ssrn.2390186

Meena, K., & Thakkar, J. (2014). Development of balanced scorecard for healthcare using interpretive structural modeling and analytic network process. *Journal of Advances in Management Research, 11*(3), 232-256. doi:10.1108/jamr-12-2012-0051

Miner-Romanoff, K. (2012). Interpretive and critical phenomenological crime studies: A model design. *Qualitative report, 17*(54), 1-32. Retrieved from http://www.nova.edu/ssss/QR/

Morrissey, M. B., Viola, D., & Shi, Q. (2014). Relationship between pain and chronic illness among seriously ill older adults: Expanding role for palliative social work. *Journal of Social Work in End-Of-Life & Palliative Care, 10*(1), 8-33. doi:10.1080/15524256.2013.877861

National Association of Public Hospitals and Health Systems. (2012). *Study reveals NAPH members are 'Providers of choice' for all patients (Research brief)*. Washington, DC: Author.

Needleman, J., & Ko, M. (2012). The declining public hospital sector. In M. Hall & S. Rosenbaum (Eds.), *The health care "safety net" in a post-reform world* (pp. 200-213). New Brunswick, NJ: Rutgers University Press.

Onwuegbuzie, A. J., Leech, N. L., & Collins, K. M. T. (2012). Qualitative analysis techniques for the review of the literature. *Qualitative Report, 17*(56), 1-28. Retrieved from http://www.nova.edu/ssss/QR/

Perla, R. J., & Provost, L. P. (2012). Judgment sampling: A health care improvement perspective. *Quality Management in Health Care, 21*, 169-175. doi:10.1097/QMH.0b013e31825e8806

Rohrer, J. E. (2014). Reinventing the case study for community health and primary care research. *Journal of Primary Care & Community Health, 5*(2), 78-79. doi:10.1177/2150131914522735

Richards, L., & Morse, J. M. (2012). *Readme first for a user's guide to qualitative methods*. Thousand Oaks, CA: Sage Publications.

Rosenberg Hansen, J., & Ferlie, E. (2014). Applying strategic management theories in public sector organizations: Developing a typology. *Public Management Review, 18*(1), 1-19. doi:10.1080/14719037.2014.957339

Sainaghi, R., Phillips, P., & Corti, V. (2013). Measuring hotel performance: Using a balanced scorecard perspectives' approach. *International Journal of Hospitality Management, 34*, 150-159. doi:10.1016/j.ijhm.2013.02.008

Saxby, R. (2013). Cutting costs without losing blood. *British Journal of Healthcare Management, 19*(7), 318-323. doi:10.12968/bjhc.2013.19.7.318

Sharpley, C. F., & Bitsika, V. (2014). Validity, reliability and prevalence of four "clinical content" subtypes of depression. *Behavioural Brain Research, 259*, 9-15. doi:10.1016/j.bbr.2013.10.032

Tarigan, J., & Widjaja, D. C. (2014). The relationship between non-financial performance and financial performance using balanced scorecard framework: A research in education context. *Journal of Economics, Business and Management, 3*, 614-618. doi:10.7763/joebm.2014.v2.96

Trotta, A., Cardamone, E., Cavallaro, G., & Mauro, M. (2013). Applying the Balanced Scorecard approach in teaching hospitals: A literature review and conceptual framework. *The International Journal of health Planning and Management, 28*(2), 181-201. doi:10.1002/hpm.2132

Verbano, C., & Crema, M. (2013). Future developments in health care performance management. *JMDH, 6*, 415-421. doi:10.2147/jmdh.s54561

Virtue, A., Chaussalet, T., & Kelly, J. (2013). Healthcare planning and its potential role increasing operational efficiency in the health sector: A viewpoint. *Journal of Enterprise Information Management, 26*(1), 8-20. doi:10.1108/17410391311289523

Wu, H. (2012). Constructing a strategy map for banking institutions with key performance indicators of the balanced scorecard. *Evaluation and Program Planning, 35*(3), 303-320. doi:10.1016/j.evalprogplan.2011.11.009

Yin, R. K. (2014). *Case study research: Design and methods* (5th ed.). Thousand Oaks, CA: Sage Publications.

About the Author...

Dr. Frank Musmar resides in Richardson, Texas. Dr. Frank is currently an adjunct professor at Louisiana International College and American Management and Technology University. Dr. Frank received his Doctorate of Business Administration (DBA) in Healthcare Management from Walden University in 2016 and a Master of Science (MS) in Biotechnology Management from the University of Maryland in 2011.

Dr. Frank is the founder and the Lead Dissertations Consultant at Editors Dissertations and Thesis, founded on the ideals that helping students achieve their educational goals could bring positive social change.

Dr. Frank is also an active member of the Delta Mu Delta Honor Society and Golden Key International Honor Society.

He has published two journal publications: *Job Embeddedness and Employee Retention in Healthcare* and a *Once-daily Oral Medication for Treatment of Cognitive Dysfunction in Down Syndrome*. Additional work includes his dissertation: *Financial Distress in the Health Care Business*.

To reach Dr. Frank Musmar for information on professional editing or guest speaking, please visit his **websites:** http://www.editorsdissertationsandthesis.com or **e-mail:** frankmusmar@gmail.com

CHAPTER 4

Managing Nonprofit Inevitable Cyber-Vulnerabilities

Dr. Avideh Sadaghiani-Tabrizi & Dr. Teresa Lao

Threats of cyber-attacks in the global economy do not exclude nonprofit organizations. A variety of open-source software collect information to extrapolate data into concise *set of algorithms* (Cashell, Jackson, Jickling, & Webel, 2004), to make decisions and to base proprietary models on underlying assumptions (Cashell et al., 2004). Exercise of a strategic approach to protect privacy and consideration to acquire liability coverage, to alleviate the effect of data breach in a digital landscape might help nonprofit organizations, in efforts with data-protection. Charitable and not-for-profit organizations' careful scrutiny to assess risks for threat of cyber-breaches might deem necessary, if a not-for-profit organization engages in the following list of three activities: (a) conduct e-commerce, such as donations tracking, registration of event, and other activities on an organization's website, (b) store personally identifiable information (PII) and sensitive personal information (SPI) of members, and transfer PIIs, or SPIs to the Internet cloud, or (c) collect habitual information about donors, or preferences and habits of patrons, and newsletter subscribers (National Council of Nonprofits, 2018).

Advances in IT revolution that consist of a series of developments in communication and processing information in digital form contribute to changes in the ways nonprofit organizations might engage in transacting on the Internet (The Levin Institute, 2014). The digital future, big data and exponential data-growth, increases in members' expectations, and the threats of a cyber-attack contribute, to not-for-profit organizational leaders' concerns over management of data and strategies. Increases in customer expectation might direct nonprofit organizations' leaders to exercise resiliency, protect data though implementation of national institute of standards (NIST) cybersecurity framework (ISO-27001), and provide a holistic approach to manage risks, proactively through a set of standards for managing the core components of security; people, processes, and technology. Adaptive-security framework incident-response plans (IRP), business-continuity plan (BCP), and intrusion-detection systems help to improve cybersecurity programs, in not-for-profit organizations to avoid malware and reduce targeted-phishing-attacks on end-users to identify and protect assets, detect and respond to threats, in exercising resiliency to recover from a breach (Ferrillo, 2015; Homeland Security, 2018). Data-security events, incidents, and the likelihood of data breaches could result in much harm to the reputation of a not-for-profit organization, categorizing in a high-priority because many unethical and bad actors might jeopardize consumer-data.

A multitude of vulnerabilities in data-security events could prompt a breach in data, in which vulnerabilities and computer network hacking could jeopardize not-for-profit organizations' reputation because nonprofits' limited resources might not suffice to address security events, as in the following: (a) loss of a laptop; (b) inadequate security and record snooping; (c) computer virus; (d) insecure disposal of sensitive information; and (e) disclosure and selling of private data (BMS Canada Risk Services Ltd., 2018). A cyber breach identifies as a data-security event, compromising individuals' confidential and, or sensitive private information, victimizing data to unauthorized and, or bad actors. Nonprofit organizations are not immune to the risk of cyber-vulnerabilities and data-breaches, requiring scrutiny to assess threat levels and safeguard for privacy of confidential data in the digital revolution that presents a cyberspace of *conceptual weaknesses* from *imperfect technologies* (BMS Canada Risk Services Ltd., 2018; Lewis, 2018). Data-security events, incidents, and the likelihood of data breaches could result in much harm to the reputation of a not-for-profit organization, categorizing data-security as high-priority because many unethical and bad actors' malicious attempts might jeopardize consumer-data. Assessment of security, together with data-loss and incident-response plans could serve organizations as invaluable to prepare for possibility of risk of threat to security (Valdetero & Zetoony, 2014).

Many not-for-profit organizations collect and store sensitive personal information that is protected by law as confidential, which could place an organization at risk of threat to members and individuals. Exploit in protected PII and SPI could place not-for-profit organizations at risk of being breached. The weakest link in security is the wetware who could fall victim to bad-actors' email-solicitation, phishing, and spear-phishing schemes. The not-for-profit organizations could be liable for failing to protect consumers, if security events, incidents, or breaches in confidentiality affirm a failure to protect the nonprofit organization's membership systems from the threats of security risks and / or protect members' data from unauthorized disclosure (Valdetero & Zetoony, 2014). Vulnerabilities lurk in the world-wide-web of the Internet, in which artificial intelligent programs use of modern technologies could disguise, parse, and analyze information (Keenan, 2014). The lack of knowledge in cybersecurity when engaging and communicating through the Internet could potentially lead to cases of misconduct, information theft, or loss of personally identifiable information (PII), necessitating greater emphasis on monitoring and exercise of aware control over Internet transmissions and Internetworking (Tabrizi, 2017).

Cybersecurity-aware internetworking could reduce the number of Internet crimes in a society where presence of IT has been changing communication and lives (DeLeo, 2008). On a similar theme from the month of October's analogy to the time to celebrate Halloween for fun, candy, and costumes, in which malware could ploy end-users through disguising in costumes to trick the end-user into installing the malware reaffirms necessity cybersecurity-aware wetware-internetworking (Tabrizi, 2017). This current national cybersecurity awareness month (NCSAM) of October 2018 commemorated the fifteenth year to bring to attention the importance of end-user's cybersecurity knowledge and awareness as an annual initiative, in raising awareness about the importance of cybersecurity. NCSAM's 2018 collaborative effort of government and industry helps to provide resources to every American to stay safe and more secure online. Accordingly, NCSAM increases the resiliency of the nation during cyber-threats, to avoid the tricks of malware costumes, such as trick or treaters, other Halloween issues, and mischief makers (Duffy, 2015).

Consequences of Cyber Breaches

Vulnerabilities in possession, access, and transmission of nonprofit organizations' data could place innocent attributes of individuals' confidential and private data at risk of unauthorized access, causing a financial burden on resources. Financial burn to the organization could vary from costs, associating with government investigation, legal and defense litigations, business interruption, award of damages to victims of breaches, and incurring expenses for notifying individuals (BMS Canada Risk Services Ltd., 2018). Hackers targeted various news and research websites to redirect visitors to an alternate site, downloading malicious code and Android package kits (APKs) (Kaspersky Lab, 2018), in which malware disguised to trick the end-users into installing the malware, instigating security events, incidents, or inevitably breaches, given the likelihood of cyber-attacks. The important role of IT is to reform and increase resources, to channel effective exchange of information for globalization (The Levin Institute, 2014). The lack of end-user's awareness of risks of threat vulnerabilities, and threat vectors could expose "the disparagement of nonprofit staff" (Brill, Land, Herrburger, Balcanoff, & Wright, 2018, p. 127), and present another layer of complexity to necessitate resolving the problems, which could harm wellbeing of the society. Refractive consideration of continual critical thinking to incorporate cyber and privacy coverage could improve nonprofit organizations' digital future and cybersecurity posture with a "comprehensive information security program" (Valdetero & Zetoony, 2014, p. vii). A focus on malicious behavior, threat vulnerabilities and the internal environment, culture, or security programs to help, in framing an emergence of a *state of compromise*, to reduce loss from loss of data or *intellectual property*, and *interruption to business operations*, which could damage the reputation of the no-for-profit organization (Raghavan, 2016).

Implementation of proactive-data-management strategies could help, in addressing threats of a cyber-attack. The ability to respond to threats requires resiliency to overcome catastrophic events. Development of an incident response plan (IRP) could help with concerns over cyber-incidents. Additionally, a crisis management plan (CMP) will help to manage innovations in artificial intelligent programs' use of modern technologies to disguise, parse, and analyze data, which necessitate nonprofit executives' awareness to address the vulnerabilities through cryptography, to address the root cause of failure. Accordingly, not-for-profit organizations rank low at twenty-percent (20%) among customers, in trusting to protect personal information, and preserving customers' privacy (Ponemon Institute, LLC, 2017). Probability to achieve perfect security in cyberspace of imperfect technologies is rare, and a response plan to security events, incidents, or breaches might benefit from counsel who would understand various elements of an attack, preparing an organization for an incident occurrence (Valdetero & Zetoony, 2014). Additionally, an awareness against spear-phishing, snooping, spyware, Trojan horse, a multitude of other online-and-self-propagating threats direct attention to strive for resiliency, in taking precautions and to encourage avoidance of threat actors. Private clouds have been providing a concept of secure-cloud computing, allowing a distinct and secure cloud-based environment for specified client to operate, accessible only by one organization to provide control over privacy (Cashell et al., 2004).

Remote statistical and monitoring systems provide feedback, in real-time. Digital health (D-Health) decisions support disruptive nature in healthcare increases savings for the hospitals, which represent modern innovations in health systems to offer *inexpensive and widespread* access to *medical data acquisition devices* through widespread availability of de-identifiable health data and analytics algorithms (Page et al., 2016, p. 18). Accordingly, Page et al. (2016), denoted improvements in accuracy of diagnostic, with a possibility to *create third party business opportunities,* which present challenges and need evaluation. Sufficient measures should "protect against cyberattacks," [in which] "contingency plan or response plan to cyberattacks" [could allow] "resources to recover from an incident" (Page et al., 2016, p. 18; Raghavan, 2016, p. 10) upon attack. The multiple elements of consideration could help not-for-profit organizations to: (a) ensure the *privacy and security* of data *acquisition, storage, and processing*; (b) consider the amount of time, the accuracy of decision support algorithms, and the size of the database, given *a large dataset for specific health conditions* could create *a natural vicious cycle.* (c) *embrace the D-Health concept* that will take time to evaluate potential *risks implied* to base decisions, effecting *human lives on machine suggestions*, (d) consider *business opportunities* of this technology, (e) consider IoT technology's infancy without a clear vision into the secure and *reliable sensing platform*, (f) consider ease and usability to visualize reliability of the data, *in a non-overwhelming summarized format to be useful to the doctors* and to embrace, and (g) consider the possibility of statistical inference from the proprietary nature of *large databases for many diseases*, for a wide variety of diseases, *detected through remote health monitoring* (Page et al., 2016, p. 18).

Evaluation of security measures for raising organizational awareness of the wetware could help to protect and ensure that data would transmit correct information. Introduction of mathematical decentralized algorithms in digital platforms' blockchain technology has been disrupting societies by mining and managing identities' "security, privacy, and usability" (Nabi, 2017, p. i), in which the improvements in securing PII contribute to the fundamental knowledge and existing theories of privacy in a dynamic hyper-convergent world. To minimize the risk of unintentional data loss or confidential information, in case of being hacked, captured, or stolen, sniffing and port-based, domain name system (DNS) and Man-In-The-Middle attacks, which could spread and persist in a hyper-connected and wireless environment (Tabrizi, Sharifzadeh, Lao, & Paluch, 2018), the process of critical thinking and development of continual new cybersecurity knowledge supports the presence of many threat vectors in a target-rich environment, crippling intellectual properties and indicative of the possibility for a breach in PII.

A PII refers to personally identifiable information of an individual, which could be available, stored, or "transmitted in any medium" (Avancha, Baxi, & Kotz, 2012, pp. 44-45). Nonprofit organizations could approach security and risks of a breach in security, proactively by incorporating the security measures to stop the attacks and cyber-offenses. Threat vectors include paths or tools that target valuable information or assets, for gaining control of a server's confidential data, computer, iPad, social media account, password, or bank account. The data input into the digital devices needs encryption to protect against loss of PII. Additionally, the information leak in credentials of some system administrators is indicative of the possibility of errors among "IT professionals and the broader workforce," [as well as] "the cybersecurity ecosystem" [who allowed] "'spear phishing' e-mail" (Ferrillo, 2015, p. 72) hook and compromise many innocent attributes. The presence of the cyberthreats requires countermeasures to reduce the risk of exposures to an attack.

Strategic Plan for Nonprofits' Internetworking

The resiliency against online malicious behavior could improve nonprofits' detection for threats of loss of PII or SPI, in the hyper-connected cyberspace against threat actors, vectors, and network attacks in an environment that overcoming barriers is essential for avoidance of stagnation (Tabrizi et al., 2018). In the world-wide-web of inter-connected the Internet, cyber-blocks could be helpful in blocking systems from inappropriate material and deviants such as worms, Trojans, porn and stalkers, and risk for harm. Accordingly, the procedures for creating a strategic plan could focus on the scope of strategic planning, including the need for the innovative strategies to resolve the problems with vulnerabilities, interoperability, and security issues with protecting confidential information through fighting in a cyber-war against the very sophisticated and organized adversaries. Internet activities monitoring and continual nonprofits' staff development, in teaching cybersecurity skills and awareness to judge Internet content could increase safe use of the Internet for communication, social networking, and conducting research in the digital-age (Tabrizi, 2017). Organizational security levels could benefit from prototypes, and building-upon the organization's transparency, in taking small steps and risks to iterate through design thinking methods as a way to identify and articulate some design thinking to rethink the avenues of attacks. Iterating through the strategic plan for implementation of secure and resilient exercises of cybersecurity could help to reduce online threats of a cyber-attack.

Challenges to Privacy in Secure Nonprofits' Internetworking

The advent of Internet increases societal demands, services, and expectations of not-for-profit organizations, in protection of members' PIIs in data-acquisition, storage, transmission, and analytics, such as: (a) IoT devices serve as a *viable technology* in data-acquisition. (b) Emerging technologies provide *system-level and cryptographic mechanisms,* to secure privacy of data-storage and transmission. (c) The emerging decision-support algorithms enable data-analytics and statistical inferences for numerical and categorical data, to perform hypothesis tests, interpret p-values, and to report the interpretable results, to explore, eliminate, or sharpen a hypothesis, to increase accuracy of decision-making about the world that can be addressed by the data. Decentralization of technologies, virtual machines, distributed-computation platform, organizing employees and resources in a mesh, rather than a hierarchy extend blockchains or chains of cryptography of blocks of information. Cloud computing's favorable-on-demand networking might necessitate resiliency to enable convenient access to flexible computing environments and resources, which configure as a shared group to allow "interaction by service provider" (Page Hijazi, Askan, Kantarci, & Soyata, 2016, p. 24).

Smartphone devices, which are "heterogeneous thin or thick platforms can reach resources through the network accessing over standard mechanisms" (Page et al., 2016, p. 24). Privacy of PII in continual collection and sharing of information with companies, websites, and social media might direct realization of the consequences for the threats, with exposure could be severe, "leading to loss of money or reputation" (Page et al., 2016, p. 19). Consideration of PII elements for securing privacy, in addition to awareness of privacy could be vital to organizational cybersecurity posture. PII consists of any combination of data points, including a specific individual's identification, the disclosure of PII such as, a name or email address, and another sensitive information that could include social security and a form of state identification, or financial account numbers of individuals. Sensitive PII could exist if PII is together with private information about an individual such as date of birth, information that pertains to medical history, or passwords, which could allow building the pieces of data about an individual, directing attention to risk of data breach. Accordingly, "cyber-blocks help to block" (Tabrizi, 2017, p. 33) deviants. The concept of privacy is about confidentiality, in keeping information secret, and individuals' rights to privacy revolve around access, accuracy, and control of the information.

Addressing Challenges with Securing Nonprofits' Internetworking

The Internet is not secure for reasons of many weaknesses, and presence of *imperfect technologies.* The communication in transmission, storage, and growth of data in approximately 50 billion Internet of Things (IoT) trackable-connected devices, with personal smartphones and then to Internet need security (Fernandez & Pallis, 2014; Hassanalieragh et al., 2015; Page et al., 2016, p. 18). Not-for-profit organizations need not to honor privacy of membership systems only, but need to protect confidentiality, using a set of principles to: (a) manage information, by collecting only on an as-need-basis to conduct business; (b) retain information for only as long as the information is necessary, destroying the information, properly; and (c) allow review of information for accuracy. Privacy involves "rights to access, correct, and control the information" of stakeholders, contributors, and users' PII and SPI (Lewis, 2018). Accordingly, "investing in information security goes beyond protecting the business" [within] "the increasingly sophisticated and interconnected global" (Raghavan, 2016, p. 13) Internet environment.

Many monitoring systems could help to identify Internet activities. Digital signatures, network system activity logs, evidence of compromise, or identification of data, showing a security-incident might help to show network anomalies to detect behaviors when looked at in the whole. A review of cybersecurity framework to develop skills, and awareness to judge Internet content could increase safe use of the Internet for communication and conducting research in the digital-age, in not-for-profit organizations. In conclusion, data is the life-blood of an organization, in which identifying organizational assets might need to invoke a good IRP, prior to a breach. Protection of the privacy of membership information systems is of the utmost responsibility, needing much care with accountability for the management, or mismanagement, of PIIs and SPIs, requiring a comprehensive information security program, in place to document administrative, technical, and physical safeguards to help protect data. Consideration of techniques as such as encryption, authentication, and sand-boxing organizational emails could help to minimize the risk of targeted cyber-attacks especially as hackers become more sophisticated (Ferrillo, 2015; Tabrizi, 2017). Resiliency to cyber incidents might be the best approach to respond to a cyber-attack and a plan of response to security events might benefit from counsel who would understand various elements of an attack, to prepare an organization for an incident occurrence. Dangers are lurking for recurrent threats with any new technology, or revitalization of an old technology within the ecosystem of digital world (Valdetero & Zetoony, 2014).

THOUGHTS FROM THE ACADEMIC ENTREPRENEUR

The problems to be solved:

- •Provide strategic solutions for securing information technologies in not-for-profit organizations to offset dollars spent on projects, cost overruns, and cancelations
- •Ineffective team leadership that influences project performance
- •Assess the new threats of modern attacks
- •Provide rapid response to technological changes, and to re-align needs to counter volatilities in technologies' disruptive nature

The goals:

- •Assess current organizational strategies to include project teams in an earlier stage of strategic planning
- •Enhance team leadership skillset when managing multiple type compositions simultaneously

The questions to ask:

- •How can nonprofit organizations be augmented to improve project team's performance?
- •How can evolvable strategies benefit organizations in various not-for-profit industries?

Today's Business Application:

- •Assess the practically of evolvability strategy in existing organizational strategies.
- •Treat team leadership as a practitioner's field and enhance skillset to accommodate managing multiple types of teams (traditional, virtual, and hybrid), concurrently.

REFERENCES

Avancha, S., Baxi, A., & Kotz, D. (2012;2013;). Privacy in mobile technology for personal healthcare. *ACM Computing Surveys (CSUR), 45*(1), 1-54. 10.1145/2379776.2379779

BMS Canada Risk Services Ltd. (2018, February 7). Cyber security and privacy risk: Vulnerability in the nonprofit and charitable sector. Charity Village. Retrieved August 14, 2018 from https://charityvillage.com/cms/content/topic/cyber_security_and_privacy_risk_vulnerability_in_the_nonprofit_and_charitable_sector/last/239#.W3MzD5LD9_M

Brill, J., Land, D., Herrburger, W., Balcanoff, K., & Wright, J. (2018). *Nonprofit and For-profit healthcare organization satisfaction based on compensation packages.* In C. Lentz (Ed.), *The refractive thinker: Volume XIV – HealthCare: The impact on leadership, business, and education* (pp. 127-144). Grayslake, IL: The Refractive Thinker® Press.

Cashell, B., Jackson, W. D., Jickling, M., & Webel, B. (2004). The economic impact of cyber-attacks. Government and Finance Division-CRS Report for Congress. Retrieved from http://www.au.af.mil/au/awc/awcgate/crs/rl32331.pdf

DeLeo, J. L. (2008, October 13). *How tech has changed our lives.* Retrieved from http://www.pcmag.com/article2/0,2817,2332339,00.asp

Duffy, T. (2015, October). Malware wears costumes, too. *Center for Internet Security, Monthly Security Tips Newsletter. Multi-State Information Sharing & Analysis Center, The Center for Internet Security* (CIS): *Stop, Think, Connect Campaign Monthly Security Tips.* Retrieved from http://msisac.cisecurity.org/newsletters/2015-10.cfm

Fernandez, F., & Pallis, G. C. (2014). Opportunities and challenges of the Internet of Things for healthcare: Systems engineering perspective. *4th International Conference on Wireless Mobile Communication and Healthcare.*

Ferrillo, P. A. (2015). Navigating cybersecurity storm: A guide for directors and officers. *Advisen, Ltd.* Retrieved from https://cybersummitusa.com/wp-content/uploads/2015/12/navigatingcybersecuritystorm-paulferrillo.pdf

Friel, A. (2011). Digital media: Handle with care. *Law Technology News.* Retrieved from http://www.law.com/jsp/lawtechnologynews/PubArticle-FriendlyLTN.jsp?id=1202536525505

Giandomenico, A. (2017). Know your enemy: Understanding threat actors. CSO: Fortinet. Retrieved from https://www.csoonline.com/article/3203804/security/know-your-enemy-understanding-threat-actors.html

Gottlieb, S., (2018). *Reflections on a landmark year for medical product innovation and public health advances and looking ahead to policy in 2018.*

[Web log comment]. Retrieved from https://blogs.fda.gov/fdavoice/index.php/2018/01/reflections-on-a-landmark-year-for-medical-product-innovation-and-public-health-advances-and-looking-ahead-to-policy-in-2018/

Haghi, M., Thurow, K., Habil, I., Stoll, R., & Habil, M. (2017, January). *Wearable devices in medical Internet of things: Scientific research and commercially available devices.* Retrieved from https://synapse.koreamed.org/DOIx.php?id=10.4258/hir.2017.23.1.4

Hart, T., Greenfield, M., MacLaughlin, S., & Geier, H. (2010). *Internet management for nonprofits: Strategies, tools and trade secrets. The AFP/Wiley Fund Development Ser. Volume 193 Edition.* Retrieved from https://ebookcentral-proquest-com.contentproxy.phoenix.edu

Hassanalieragh, M., Page, A., Soyata, T., Sharma, G., Aktas, M., Mateos, G., Kantarci, B., Andreescu, S. (2015). Health monitoring and management using Internet-of-Things (IoT) sensing with cloud-based processing: Opportunities and challenges. doi:10.1109/GLOCOM.2015.7417414. Dept. of ECE, Univ. of Rochester, Rochester, NY, Clarkson Univ., Postdam, NY, USA. *IEEE International Conference on Services Computing (SCC)*, (pp. 285-292). New York, NY.

Homeland Security. (2018). *Official website of the Department of Homeland Security: National cybersecurity awareness month.* Retrieved from https://www.dhs.gov/national-cyber-security-awareness-month

Keenan, T. P. (2014). *Techno creep: The surrender of privacy and the capitalization of intimacy.* New York, NY: OR Books.

Keller, J. (2015, September 18). *Air Force reaches out to industry for ways to ensure communications in nuclear events.* Retrieved from http://www.militaryaerospace.com/articles/2015/09/nuclear-military-communications.html

Kaspersky Lab. (2018, May). *Who's who in the zoo: Cyberespionage operation targets Android users in the Middle East.* Retrieved from https://media.kasperskycontenthub.com/wp-content/uploads/sites/43/2018/05/03114450/ZooPark_for_public_final_edit.pdf

Krumm, J. (2010). *Ubiquitous computing fundamentals.* Boca Raton, FL: CRC Press.

Lewis, J.A. (2018, January). *Rethinking cybersecurity: Strategy, mass effect, and states.* Retrieved from https://csis-prod.s3.amazonaws.com/s3fs-public/publication/180108_Lewis_ReconsideringCybersecurity_Web.pdf

Lohrmann, D. (2018, September). New national cyber strategy message: Deterrence through U.S. strength. Government Technology. Retrieved from http://www.govtech.com/blogs/lohrmann-on-cybersecurity/new-national-cyber-strategy-message-deterrence-through-us-strength.html?utm_term=READ%20MORE&utm_campaign=Digital%20States%20Survey%202018%3A%20Raising%20the%20Bar%2C%20FirstNet%20Names%20

New%20Acting%20CEO&utm_content=email&utm_source=Act-On+Software&utm_medium=email

Messdaghi, C., (2017, October). *Nonprofits cannot ignore cybersecurity.* [Web log comment]. Retrieved from https://blog.kennasecurity.com/2017/10/nonprofits-cannot-ignore-cybersecurity/

Muck, S. (2012). Safeguarding PII on shared drives continues to be a challenge. *CHIPS Magazine, 30*(1), 13. Retrieved from https://www.hsdl.org/?view&did=11740

Nabi, A. (2017). *Comparative study on identity management methods using blockchain.* Retrieved from https://files.ifi.uzh.ch/CSG/staff/Rafati/ID%20Management%20using%20BC-Atif-VA.pdf

National Council of Nonprofits (2018). Cybersecurity for nonprofits. *National voice. State focus. Local impact.* Retrieved from https://www.councilofnonprofits.org/tools-resources/cybersecurity-nonprofits

New York State Division of Criminal Justice Services. (2010, December 29). *Child sexual predators: The familiar stranger: DCJS releases video to help parents protect their children from sexual predators* [Video file]. Retrieved from http://criminaljustice.state.ny.us/pio/video/child-sexual-predators12-29-2010-hq.wmv

O'Dowd, E. (2018, February). *What are the top healthcare blockchain growing pains?* Retrieved from https://hitinfrastructure.com/news/what-are-the-top-healthcare-blockchain-growing-pains

Page, A., Hijazi, S., Askan, D., Kantarci, B., & Soyata, T. (2016). Research directions in cloud-based decision support systems for health monitoring using Internet-of-things driven data acquisition. *International Journal of Services Computing , 4,* 18-34.

Ponemon Institute, LLC. (2017, May). *The impact of data breaches on reputation & share value - A study of marketers, IT practitioners and consumers in the United Kingdom.* Centrify. Retrieved from https://www.centrify.com/media/4772757/ponemon_data_breach_impact_study_uk.pdf

Prayitno, A., Subanji, & Muksar, M. (2016, May-June). *Critical thinking decision refractive thinking with dual strategy in solving mathematics problem.* Department of Mathematics Education, Universitas Wisnuwardhana Malang, Indonesia Department of Mathematics, Universitas Negeri Malang, Indonesia. *IOSR Journal of Research & Method in Education (IOSR-JRME), 6*(3), 49-56. Retrieved from https://www.academia.edu/29552493/Refractive_Thinking_with_Dual_Strategy_in_Solving_Mathematics_Problem

Raghavan, K. (2016, March-April). Cybersecurity in small businesses and nonprofit organizations. *Tech Issues: Today's CPA.* Retrieved from https://www.tscpa.org/docs/default-source/default-document-library/cybersecurity-marapril16-(1).pdf?sfvrsn=2

Rosenbaum, M. H. (2015). *Identifying unethical personally identifiable information (PII) privacy violations committed by IS/IT practitioners: A comparison to computing moral exemplars* (Doctoral dissertation). Retrieved from ProQuest Dissertations & Theses Global. (UMI No. 1658171258)

Sodiya, A. S., & Adegbuyi, B. (2016). A framework for protecting users' privacy in cloud. *International Journal of Information Security and Privacy (IJISP), 10*(4), 33-43. 10.4018/IJISP.2016100102

Tabrizi, A. S. (2017). *Integrating cybersecurity education in K-6 curriculum: Schoolteachers, IT experts, and parents' perceptions.* Dissertation, University of Phoenix.

Tabrizi, A. S.., Sharifzadeh, M., Lao, T., & Paluch, E. (2018). PII and PHI's privacy in a dynamic hyper-convergent world. In C. Lentz (Ed.), *The refractive thinker®: Volume XIV: HealthCare: The impact on leadership, business, and education* (pp. 51-69). Grayslake, IL: The Refractive Thinker® Press.

The Levin Institute. (2014). *Information technology.* Retrieved from http://www.globalization101.org/information-technology

Tapscott, D., & Tapscott, A. (2016). *Blockchain revolution.* Retrieved from http://blockchain-revolution.com

Valdetero, J., & Zetoony, D. (2014). Data security breaches: Incident preparedness and response. Bryan Cave LLP. Washington Legal Foundation©2014. Retrieved from https://www.bryancave.com/images/content/2/2/v2/2285/DataBreachHandbookValdeteroandZetoony.pdf

About the Authors...

Dr. Avideh Sadaghiani-Tabrizi is from the Capital Region in upstate New York and holds several accredited degrees: a Doctorate of Management (DM) in Organizational Leadership with Specialization in Information Systems Technology (DM / IST) and a Master of Science in Computer Information Systems (MS / CIS) from the School of Advanced Studies of the University of Phoenix. Dr. Avideh Tabrizi is an Information Systems Technology Specialist II (Programmer) at the Office of Information Technology Services – Health & Human Services cluster, Application Development, and Support Group, participating in design, development, and maintenance of a web-based electronic database system with over 20 years of service at the New York State government. She enjoys travelling and likes to engage in various physical fitness activities when possible.

Dr. Avideh Tabrizi serves on North Colonie Central School District-Board of Education, participating in decision making, monitoring, and conducting reviews of the school district's curriculums, policies, and budget, in addition to serving as the president of high school's parents, teachers, and students' association. Her doctoral study entitled *Integrating Cybersecurity Education in K-6 Curriculum: Schoolteachers, IT Experts, and Parents' Perceptions*, provided her the opportunity to gain a deeper understanding about academic needs of children, to suggest and facilitate improvements in the school district.

To reach Dr. Avideh Tabrizi, please **e-mail: avideh2012@yahoo.com**

Dr. Teresa Lao holds several accredited degrees: a Doctorate of Philosophy (Ph.D) from New Mexico State University and a Master of Arts (MA) from Ball State University with qualitative research study interests in curriculum and instructions methods, distance learning, curriculum & instruction, technology integration, women and leadership roles, education, learning technologies, higher education, women's issues, leadership, and organization.

Dr. Teresa is a curriculum and course developer for business, writing, and foundations courses while serving as a consultant for the Academic Council on Education to review military courses for college credits. Her work experience includes Equal Employment Opportunity investigator, where she investigated discrimination complaints, newspaper copy editor for the El Paso Times, writing lab reviewer, and GED / ESL instructor. Dr. Lao is pursuing an Executive Juris Doctorate, as of the date of this publication, to broaden her knowledge of the law. Dr. Teresa believes in the importance of lifelong, and that knowledge is within our reach. We need to take the initiative to improve our current skill.

Dr. Teresa is a published author in several peer-reviewed journals, including the *Journal of Technology and Teacher Education, Global Journal of Business Research, and Journal of Leadership Studies.*

To reach Dr. Teresa Lao, please **e-mail: drteresalao@yahoo.com**

CHAPTER 5

A Critical Perspective on Selection Practices in Texas Community Colleges

Dr. Barbara J. Yancy-Tooks

A vast amount of literature documents barriers experienced by women in accession to senior leadership positions in higher education (Patitu & Hinton, 2003; Graham, 2015; Studvent, 2017). The scarcity of African American women in top leadership positions in Texas community colleges provided the drive to explore this phenomenon and document progress. Previous researchers had not explored selection practices as a factor contributing to the low representation of African American women in senior academic levels of leadership. Additionally, very little is known about the experiences of African American female academic leaders in community college administration specifically, in Texas community colleges (Yancy-Tooks, 2012). The focus of this chapter is to broaden knowledge about women's experiences and perceptions regarding selection practices. Using strategies provided in The Refractive Thinker® will help to increase awareness and understanding of leadership development initiatives needed to affect change.

Background

Progress in accession to higher levels of academic leadership continues at a slow pace for African American women and the challenges that they faced are well documented. Female senior administrative leaders advanced however, barriers persist on impeding progression into positions at community colleges (Bailey, 2009; Chock; 2007; De Los Santos, 2008; Donahue-Mendoza 2012; Fisher; 2008; Flannigan, Jones, & Moore, 2004; Gill, 2010; Gill & Jones, 2013; Graham, 2015, Studvent, 2016). Researchers emphasized the importance of documenting factors either facilitating or impeding progress that discourage African American women who desire to advance in higher education (Duree, 2007; Moses, 2014; Hague, 2016). Conversely, the literature about barriers experienced by African American women is unclear about how the barriers affect women's decisions to continue or not continue the pursuit into higher leadership positions (Braxton, 2018). No single factor exists that influences advancement of Black women into higher education, however a close examination of persistent obstacles is warranted to develop policies to encourage participation in higher education administration (Bailey, 2009; Studvent, 2016).

The low representation of women in education administration is significant to Texas. Previous research addressed stumbling blocks that Hispanic women encountered in reaching higher level positions in Texas community colleges (De Los Santos, 2008). Researchers also explored the strong male-controlling influences contributing to the marginalization of four community college female administrators in West Texas (Gill & Jones, 2013). However, the voices of African American women aspiring to reach higher education administrative positions in Texas community colleges is absent from the literature (Yancy-Tooks, 2012). The perception of marginalization is another reason African American women are underrepresented in presidency positions in community colleges (Studvent, 2016). Research investigating the indiscernible presence of African American women administrators in the community college is scarce (Graham, 2015). The presence of Black women on campus and in leadership positions provides advocacy for Black women students. They also serve as mentors, role models and channels of support (Moses, 2014).

Meeting the needs of students from ethnically diverse backgrounds requires a diverse faculty and staff (Lopez, 2006). In Texas, the minority student population is increasing (Murdock et al., 2003; National Center for Education Statistics (NCES), 2017; Waller & Hase, 2004). There are 128 community colleges (80 public colleges and 48 private colleges) throughout the state of Texas (Community College Review, n.d.). During the 2018 and 2019 school year 775,525 students enrolled (Community College Review, n.d.). A report from the American Association of Community Colleges (AACC, 2018) showed the student population in Texas is 4% Asian, 37% Hispanic, 13% Black, and White 39%. However, compared to students attending community colleges, faculty, and staff are not as diverse (AACC, 2018). Managers and leaders must adapt to a changing society in response to working with diverse groups. New approaches and a needs assessment of organizational practices will increase leader effectiveness (Chin, 2010).

Three Lenses: Organizational, Systems, and Critical

An analysis of the experiences and perceptions of African American women in Texas community college administration required a refractive thinking approach. Thus, organizational theory, systems theory and critical theory provided a framework to broaden the analysis. Three aspects of the community college organization explored assisted in gaining an understanding of first, the decision making capacity and cultural behavior (Scott & Davis 2007; Schein, 2008). Second, making the connection between culture and values (Bierma, 2003). Third, assessing perceptions of power based upon marginalized groups in society (Crotty, 2004).

Recognizing barriers, practices, and factors contributing to the marginalization of African American women is essential to preparing other women leaders in the future (Williams, 2009). The lack of supervisory support poses another barrier to advancement (Donahue-Mendoza, 2012). Donahue-Mendoza (2012) examined supervision as factor facilitating or impeding career advancement of mid-level managers. Using a sample of two focus groups from the West Valley Community College District in California, the researcher reported that ineffective supervision from the executive leadership adversely affected career progression. Poor supervision and the lack of guidance resulted in ignoring women's potential, lack of formal training for a supervisory role, and the absence of support for pursuing higher education and training opportunities (Donahue-Mendoza, 2012).

Societal Barriers Hindering Advancement

Miller and Vaughn (1997) explored the experiences and difficulties faced by African American women executives in a variety of professions. Forty participants from the fields of higher education, business, law, and medicine participated in the study. Miller and Vaughn (1997) found that race and gender bias were most prevalent in the workplace. Based on the perceptions of others in the workplace, women were incapable, intellectually inferior, and underprepared (Miller & Vaughn, 1997). Gender inequity is a major factor contributing to the underrepresentation of women in higher education (Smith, Altbach & Lomotey, 2002). According to Smith et al. (2002), small numbers of women, African American women specifically, held positions in the lower levels of educational administration and in the faculty ranks.

Much like refractive thinking, educational leaders continue to create intervention strategies to further address gender inequality in higher education. The American Council on Education (ACE) began a campaign in 2016 called *Moving the Needle: Advancing Women in Higher Education Leadership Initiative* (The American

Council on Education [ACE], 2016). The purpose of the initiative is two-fold: (a) to heighten awareness on a national level about the urgent need to attain gender equality and diversity in higher education leadership and (b) to find strategies for achieving equal representation of women in senior leadership positions (ACE, 2016). Gillett (2017) believed women community college leaders of color remain stagnant due to race and gender inequality. Inequality persists for African American women in top ranks of higher education (Davis & Maldonado, 2015).

Institutional Practices

Research shows specific examples of coping techniques shared by women senior level administrators (Williams, 2009). In a multi-case study that included three community college administrators located in the southern region of the United States, Williams (2009) sought to discover positive factors regarding the advancement of African American women into upper-level community college administration. William's research highlighted coping strategies to include a strong spiritual foundation and awareness, the willingness to influence outcomes through collaboration and support systems from family and peers. Williams suggested when replicating the study to use a larger sample population to compare whether similarly held perspectives exist among women holding positions as Deans and Directors. African American women who persist in ascending to senior administrative positions have developed strategies for coping in academe (Hall, Everett, & Hamilton-Mason, 2012; Williams, 2009). Hall et al. (2012) suggested workplace stressors for African American women linked to racism and sexism. The following themes emerged from the research: (a) Being hired or promoted in the workplace, (b) defending one's race and lack of mentorship, (c) Shifting or code switching to overcome barriers to employment, (d) coping with racism and discrimination, and (e) being isolated and / or excluded. Coping mechanisms used adapt to workplace stressors included spirituality, physical activity and supportive relationships (Hall et al., 2012).

De Los Santos (2008) explored barriers experienced by Hispanic women administrators. The study incorporated an ethnographic design and data collection method that included interviews. Findings of strong cultural beliefs, lack of opportunity, and lack of commitment to diversifying institutions contributed to the low representation of Hispanic females in community colleges and higher education (De Los Santos, 2008).

Gill and Jones (2013) investigated women administrators in West Texas community colleges. Noting the gap in the literature, they examined how women dealt with adversity in their environment, preferred leadership styles, and women's mentoring opportunities. Gill and Jones (2013) used a case study design using a naturalistic inquiry approach, and collected data through semi-structured interviews, observation, and document analysis. Women in the study described how the culture of the workplace environment and the deeply held values of Board members kept others from seeing women as capable of success in dealing with the demands of community college administrative positions. Findings revealed that discriminatory practices against women were still prevalent, and that men outnumbered women in senior leadership positions locally and statewide (Gill & Jones, 2013). The increased presence of women in community college leadership positions shaped a cultural change reducing many of the obstacle's women encountered in the past (Gill & Jones, 2013).

Key Factors

Numerous factors became apparent when interviewing women leaders about their experiences in higher education administration. I interviewed nine African American women Administrators from various Texas community colleges to help understand their perceptions of factors hindering or facilitating advancement into community college administration. The following nine themes emerged from an analysis of the interview data: factors influencing advancement; supportive relationships in current position, professional experiences, selection and hiring processes are in place, perception that selection practices are fair, perceptions that selection practices inhibit fairness, local leadership development programs lack mentoring and preparation, personal barriers hindering advancement, and perceived barriers hindering African American women (Yancy-Tooks, 2012).

Graham (2015) investigated the experiences, challenges, and coping strategies of four African American administrators at the Community Colleges of Illinois. Various obstacles continued to adversely impact African American women's ascent to education administration positions. Factors African American women used to persist in their leadership roles included supportive team, supportive colleagues, mentoring, shifting, reducing work hours, and demonstrated competence (Graham, 2015). Highlighted below are four themes to include factors influencing advancement, supportive relationships, factors inhibiting fairness, perceived barriers and coping strategies (Yancy-Tooks, 2012).

Factors Influencing Advancement

Participants averred that preparation proved critical in their rise through the leadership ranks. All participants believed experience coupled with preparation influenced advancement opportunity. Participant 4 believed that her corporate experience influenced her advancement. "Coming from a background corporate America made a big difference." Participant 8 stated, "I think factors such as professional development, taking advantage of any opportunity, or actually searching for those things and being intentional and purposeful in the advancement." Women who aspire to senior levels of leadership in community colleges must prepare for the position (Bailey, 2009; Critchlow, 2005; Duree, 2007; Latimore, 2009; Schmitz, 2008; Studvent, 2016; Williams, 2009).

Supportive Relationships

Participants 4, 6, and 9 identified support received by specific individuals within the organization such as the president, dean of instruction, and chancellor. P9 stated, "I receive encouragement and support from students, faculty, staff, and administrators."

P2 believed that participation on committees and professional development training were supportive factors. "If you do not have the right supervisor, your career is dead in the water. You must have the opportunity to serve on committees on your campus, on your district, and at the state and national levels." P5 shared similar comments and stated that mentors, opportunities, and experience were supportive factors.

Previous research emphasized that lack of support can have a negative impact for African American women once hired into positions of leadership (Burney, 2007; Fisher, 2008). Differences in the organizational culture, organizational climate, and differences in women's experiences can contribute to the variation in responses found in this study. Based on the participants' responses to this question it seems that the support women received was the result of a positive organizational climate. Townsend and Twombly (2007) postulated that although the community college climate is favorable for women, the degree to which the community college promotes equity in the workplace environment is unclear. As minorities and women in senior leadership positions increase, reassurance, and support is necessary for minority women to achieve and excel in these positions (Gill, 2010; Graham, 2015; Latimore, 2009; Schmitz, 2008).

Factors Inhibiting Fairness

P2 indicated that implementing policies and procedures for hiring differs in practice. She stated, "The process is as fair as far as policies and procedures on paper. However, people implementing the policies and procedures have a different perception of how to apply them, and I do not know how you can regulate that." P5 said, "From my experience a lot of it has to do with who you know and politics and connections." P4 agreed, "In actual practice, educational institutions are very political, and in practice politics enters into the actual determination of who may receive the position."

P7 stated:

> I am happy to say there is a process in place, but I cannot say that that process is necessarily followed. My perception? That the process sucks, it is full of flaws; that it is more political than it is anything else; I find that it is still the good old boy network in place, even though the good old boys cease to exist, as we knew them back in the '70s when I came here.

P6 believed that the practices were fair, however implementation of the practices may not be fair for the best qualified individuals to obtain a position. "I believe that they are fair. I do but I believe that ensuring that we have representation for our race and ethnicity is concerned, sometimes overrules the best qualified person." P2, agreed, "I think oftentimes race is a major factor and it does overrule best qualified individuals." Participants 3 and 9 cited challenges in the interview process and indicated that salary and titles were not commensurate with the position upon promotion. P3 stated:

> I applied for the position, there was a formal interview process. I was in competition with people from within the institution, as well as externally, and I got the position. I got in and I did not

receive an increase in salary going from a counselor to the director of financial aid. The administration did not want to change the title to director.

P9 noted a similar experience, "they changed the title, but still there was no increase in pay." When attempting to fit in and adapt to norms established by higher education institutions, African American women faced many barriers (Bailey, 2009). Faculty and administrators of color encountered discrimination and exclusion at community colleges. Minorities and women their capabilities and talent were excluded by the individuals in power who created the community college (Jones-Kavalier & Flannigan, 2008). The inclusion of minorities and women in higher education requires institutional leaders to eliminate institutional practices excluding and marginalizing women and minority faculty by employing proactive strategies (ACE, n.d.; Evans & Chun, 2007a).

Perceived Barriers

Participants 1, 7, and 8 believed that a perception of African American women to look and act a certain way to meet other's expectations is a barrier hindering advancement. P1 asserted:

> I think that people feel that African American women, have a better chance of getting ahead and they are much more comfortable with African American women than they are with African American males. People have preconceived ideas of what it is that they want. One of the things that I find, that I am surprised about is that we are not schizophrenic, because women must act one way.

P7 agreed, "One, trying to be what you think people want you to be, particularly what White people you to be." P8 concurred, "This business of allowing people to define you, could be a hindrance. We should never do that." These findings support the literature where gender inequity is prevalent in the organizational culture (Dear, 2016; Latimore, 2009; Miller & Vaughn, 1997).

Coping Strategies

Many participants in the study offered a variety of coping strategies found in the literature to include spiritual awareness, preparation, mentoring, and family support (Steel, 2016; Williams, 2009). Previous research emphasized that coping strategies are integral to staying prepared to meet the challenges for roles of leadership in higher education administration (Williams, 2009).

P2 averred:

Find you some people that will support you and that will advise you, both formally and informally. One of the things I have learned that we do not do, when I say, "we," I mean African American, and I am going to say specifically women, we do not network with each other.

P3 stated, "I think the biggest support I had was from my family who really believed in me." P7 commented on the importance of preparation for coping in academe, "I just think it is so important that we do our homework and that we think long-term, futuristic." P1 said, "God has purposed for us what his plan is. I read the bible every morning because I never know what awaits me when I go to work."

Conclusion

Previous research that examined the underrepresentation of African American women in community college administration had not explored perceptions of selection practices from the administrator's perspective (Yancy-Tooks, 2012). The chapter provided women leader's testimonies to gain insight into lack of knowledge about the perceptions of the selection practices from the perspectives of nine African American women senior administrators at Texas community colleges. Selection practices and institutional practices contributed substantially to the perceptions of inequitable policies and the marginalization of women in higher education positions. Chapter content enhanced knowledge and understanding of the persistent barriers by sharing information about minority women in community college administration, specifically Texas community colleges. Research uncovered perceptions of factors that might contribute to the low representation of African American women in senior administrative positions. I recommend continuing the documentation and reporting of recurrent issues pertaining to the advancement of African American women in community college administration.

THOUGHTS FROM THE ACADEMIC ENTREPRENEUR

The problem to be solved:

- Identifying barriers not previously identified in the literature pertaining to career advancement of African American women in community college administration
- Reduce barriers to accession to higher administrative levels

The goals:

- Examine underrepresentation of African American women and selection practices through diverse perspectives
- Continue examining the experiences and perceptions of African American women in senior levels of leadership about institutional and selection practices
- Archive a list of coping strategies used to advance in community college administration in Texas community colleges

The questions to ask:

- How can women in higher education organizations prepare effectively?
- How does one determine new strategies to address cultural and organizational climate issues to create a positive organizational culture for advancement opportunities?

Today's Business Application:

- Supportive leaders who recognize barriers to accession can mitigate obstacles and open paths to top levels to retain women.
- The global landscape is changing, thus educational leaders must adapt to keep pace.
- Leaders must be committed to reducing the impact of race and gender inequality.

REFERENCES

American Association of Community Colleges (AACC). (2018, June 18). Faculty and staff diversity. Retrieved from https://www.aacc.nche.edu/wp-content/uploads/2018/06/DataPoints_V6N7.pdf

American Council on Education (ACE) (n.d.). ACE launches Moving the Needle Campaign to achieve higher education leadership gender parity. Retrieved from https://www.acenet.edu/news-room/Pages/ACE-Launches-Moving-the-Needle-Campaign-to-Achieve-Higher-Education-Leadership-Gender-Parity.aspx

Bailey, G. (2009). *Career advancement: A study of Black American women administrators in higher education* (Doctoral dissertation). Retrieved from ProQuest Dissertations and Theses database. (UMI No. 3320810)

Bierma, L. (2003). Systems thinking: A new lens for old problems. *Journal of Continuing Education in the Health Professions, 23* suppl-1S27-S33. doi:10.1002/chp.1340230407

Braxton, P. (2018). *Brave and fearless: African American women navigating the pathway to a community college presidency* (Doctoral dissertation). Retrieved from ProQuest Dissertations and Thesis database. (UMI No. 10824268)

Chin, J. (2010). Introduction to the special issue on diversity and leadership. *American Psychologist, 65*(3), 150-156. doi:10.1037/a0018716

Chock, S. Y. M. (2007). *Three community college pathfinders: Women of color student affairs leaders* (Doctoral dissertation). Retrieved from ProQuest Dissertations and Theses database. (UMI No. 3258065)

Community College Review. (n.d.). Top Texas community colleges. Retrieved from https://www.communitycollegereview.com/Texas

Crotty, M. (2004). *The foundations of social research: Meaning and perspective in the research process.* Thousand Oaks, CA: Sage.

Davis, D., & Maldonado, C. (2015). Shattering the glass ceiling: The leadership development of African American women in higher education. *Advancing Women in Leadership, 35,* 48-64. Retrieved from https://digitialscholarship.unlv.edu/evpp_fac_articles_/2/

De Los Santos, R. (2008). *A qualitative ethnographic study of barriers experienced by Hispanic female administrators in higher education* (Doctoral dissertation). Retrieved from ProQuest Dissertations and Theses database. (UMI No. 3323344)

Dear, R. W. (2016). *Surviving at the top: A critical case study of female administrators in higher education* (Doctoral dissertation, Georgia Southern

University). Available from Electronic Thesis and dissertation databased. https://digitalcommons.georgiasouthern.edu/etd/1488

Donahue-Mendoza, M. (2012). The supervision and career advancement of women in community college administration. *Journal of Applied Research in the Community College, 19*(2), 38. Retrieved from https://www.learntechlib.org/i/ISSN-1068-610x/v/9/n/2/

Duree, C. (2007). *The challenges of the community college presidency in the new millennium: Pathways, preparation, competencies, and leadership programs needed to survive* (Doctoral dissertation). Retrieved from ProQuest Dissertations and Theses database. (UMI No. 3289420)

Evans, A., & Chun, E. B. (2007a). The theoretical framework: Psychosocial Oppression and Diversity. *ASHE Higher Education Report, 33*(1), 1-26. doi:10.1002/ehe.3301

Fisher, J. (2008). *Career barriers experienced by midlevel women administrators at Maryland community colleges: A phenomenological study* (Doctoral dissertation). Retrieved from ProQuest Dissertations and Theses database (UMI No. 3381835)

Gill, K. M. (2010). *Women in community college administration: A west Texas perspective* (Doctoral dissertation, Texas Tech University). Retrieved from https://dspace.lib.ttu.edu/etd/handle/2346/ETD-TTU-2010-08-859

Gill, K., & Jones, S. J. (2013). Fitting in: Community college female executive leaders share their experiences--A study in west Texas. *Journal about Women in Higher Education, 6*(1), 48-70. doi:10.1515/njawhe-2013-0004

Gillett, K. R. (2017). Changing leadership: Taking a stand by "Moving the Needle" for women's leadership in community colleges. *New Directions for Community Colleges, 2017*(179), 35–45. doi:10.1002/cc.20260

Graham, M. A. (2015). *African American women administrators at the community colleges of Illinois: An investigation of obstacles and persistence* (Doctoral dissertation). Retrieved from ProQuest Dissertations and Theses database. (UMI No. 3739510)

Hague, L. Y. (2016) *Factors that impact the career advancement of African American women in higher education leadership: A focus on community colleges in North Carolina* (Doctoral dissertation). Retrieved from ProQuest Dissertations and Theses database. (UMI No. 10240406)

Hall, C. J., Everett, J. E., & Hamilton-Mason, J. (2012). Black women talk about workplace stress and how they cope. *Journal of Black Studies, 43*(2), 207–226. doi:101177/0021934711413272

Jones-Kavalier, B., & Flannigan, S. (2008). *The hiring game: Reshaping community college practices.* American Association of Community Colleges. Washington, DC: Community College Press.

Latimore, R. S. (2009). *Rising to the top: A national study of Black community college presidents* (Doctoral dissertation, University of Georgia). Retrieved from https://getd.libs.uga.edu/pdfs/latimore_robbie_s_200905_edd/latimore_robbie_s_200905_edd.pdf

Lopez, J. (2006). *The impact of demographic changes on United States higher education. 2000-2050*. State Higher Education Executive Offices. Boulder, Colorado: SHEEO Press. Retrieved from http://www.sheeo.org/pubs/demographics-lopez.pdf

Miller, J., & Vaughn, G. (1997). African American women executives: Themes that bind. In L. Benjamin (Ed.), *African American women in the academy: Promises and perils* (pp. 179-188). Gainesville, FL: University Press of Florida.

Moses, Y. T. (2014). *Black women in academe: Issues and strategies. Project on the status and education of women*. Washington, DC: Association of American Colleges and Universities. Retrieved from http://www.eric.ed.gov/PDFS/ED311817.pdf

Murdock, S., White, S., Hogue, M., Pecotte, B., You, X., & Balkin, J. (2003). *The new Texas challenge: Population change and the future of Texas*. College Station, TX: Texas A & M University Press.

National Center for Education Statistics. (2017). *Status and trends in the education of racial and ethnic groups*. Retrieved from https://nces.ed.gov/pubs2017/2017051.pdf

Patitu, C., & Hinton, K. (2003). The experiences of African American Women faculty and Administrators in higher education: Has anything changed? *New Directions for Student Services,* (104), 79-93. doi:10.1002/ss.109

Schein, E. H. (2008). *Organizational culture and leadership* (4th ed.). San Francisco: CA. Jossey-Bass.

Scott, W. R., & Davis, G. F. (2007). *Organizations and organizing: Rational, natural, and open system perspectives*. Upper Saddle River, NJ: Prentice Hall.

Schmitz, G. (2008). *Leadership preparation and career pathways of community college presidents* (Doctoral dissertation). Retrieved from ProQuest Dissertations and Theses database. (UMI No. 3307078)

Steel, L. D. (2016). *Exploring mentoring and career advancement: A community college case study* (Doctoral dissertation). Retrieved from ProQuest Dissertation and Theses database. (UMI No. 10153557)

Studvent, L. (2016). *A narrative inquiry of African American women's experience aspiring to presidency in a career college* (Doctoral dissertation). Retrieved from ProQuest Dissertation and Theses database. (UMI No. 10148323)

Townsend, B., & Twombly, S. (2007). Accidental equity: The status of women in the community college. *Equity & Excellence in Education, 40*(3), 208-217. doi:10.1080/10665680701334777

Waller, L. R., & Hase, K. N. (2004). The Texas dilemma: the ethnic gaps widen. *The Community College Enterprise, 10*(2), 79-89. Retrieved from https://www.questia.com/library/p436176/community-college-enterprise/i2510087/vol-10-no-2-fall

Williams, M. (2009). *Factors that contribute to the career ascendancy of African American female administrators* (Doctoral dissertation). Retrieved from ProQuest Dissertations and Theses database. (UMI No. 3351419)

Yancy-Tooks, B. (2012). *Impact of selection practices on career advancement of African American women in community college administration* (Doctoral dissertation). Retrieved from ProQuest Dissertations and Theses database. (UMI No. 3510599)

About the Author...

Dr. Barbara J. Yancy-Tooks resides in El Paso, Texas. Dr. Barbara culminated her military career from the U.S. Army with 21 years of service. Dr. Barbara has a Doctor of Management (DM) degree with an emphasis in Organizational Leadership from University of Phoenix School of Advanced Studies and a Master of Arts degree in Communication from the University of Northern Colorado. Dr. Barbara is an adjunct professor on faculty with Park University and University of Phoenix. Dr. Barbara served as Professor and Coordinator for the Speech Discipline at El Paso Community College Northwest Campus for 14 years. Dr. Barbara also serves as an assistant professor with the U.S. Army Sergeants Major Academy.

Dr. Barbara's awards include: The National Institute for Staff and Organizational Development (NISOD) Excellence Award Recipient (2014) and is a founding member of the El Paso Community College Teachership Academy. Dr. Barbara holds the certification for Effective College Instruction awarded by the Association of College and University Educators and the American Council on Education (ACUE).

To reach Dr. Barbara J. Yancy-Tooks, please **email** her at **byancyto@gmail.com**

CHAPTER 6

Strategies to Reduce Employee Turnover in Higher Education

Dr. Denise J. La Salle & Dr. Alexandro Beato

Global competition is a significant challenge that business leaders face daily. To gain a competitive edge over the competition, leaders must implement effective employee retention strategies. One of the best ways to increase organizational performance is by retaining top performers (Belke & Keil, 2016; Rathi & Lee, 2015). The Bureau of Labor Statistics (2015) defined turnover as the departure of employees from a workplace. The consequences to losing competent workers entail investing time recruiting new employees, reduced productivity and profitability, and spending over $3,000 on recruiting expenses per employee (Bandura & Lyons, 2014). It is crucial for nonprofit organizational leaders to understand that reducing employee turnover is necessary to increase organizational performance (Ramlall, Al-Sabaan, & Magbool, 2014).

In nonprofit higher education, leaders continue to struggle to retain employees because of the absence of a business standpoint (Samuel & Chipunza, 2013). Increased employee turnover has numerous consequences that affect nonprofit higher education organizations, team relationships, workplace efficiency, safety, and productivity (Li & Jones, 2013). Mok (2014) found that employee turnover and retention are the two most important elements that effects sustainability. The success of any institution depends on its leaders' ability to recognize that employees retention is vital to the survival of the organization (Yahaya & Ebrahim, 2016). By using a refractive thinking approach, nonprofit higher education leaders can gain new insight on effective strategies to reduce employee turnover.

Background of Employee Turnover

Educational leaders need to formulate business strategies to reduce employee turnover (Chahal & Bakshi, (2015). In addition, higher education leaders and college administrators need to acknowledge that managing nonprofit higher education organizations requires the similar skills as other business sectors (Shahrill, 2014). Researchers found that higher education administrators are having difficulty retaining skilled workers (Bandura & Lyons, 2014; Samuel & Chipunza, 2013). Losing skilled employees reduces productivity, which has an adverse effect on the financial performance of nonprofit organizations (Selesho & Naile, 2014).

To promote a high-quality learning environment, educational leaders need to manage employee retention (Samuel & Chipunza, 2013). In the educational sector, a need exists for experienced leaders who understand the importance of employee retention to efficiently manage educational institutions (Samuel & Chipunza, 2013). Educational leaders who are not effective at reducing employee turnover have a disadvantageous effect on sustainability, survivability, and productivity, which leads to an unproductive operational environment (Samuel & Chipunza, 2013).

Understanding Employee Turnover

Employee turnover is the involuntary or voluntary action of leaving one's job (Sun & Wang, 2016). Employee turnover affects companies as the result of accrued expenses from training costs, administrative fees, and recruitment (Sun & Wang, 2016; Tschoop, Grote, & Gerber, 2014). Voluntary turnover is more disruptive to an organization because when employees leave voluntarily, managers might have limited time to replace the vacancy (Sun & Wang, 2016). Contrary to voluntary turnover, involuntary turnover refers to firing an employee. In this case, administrators must decide if the time is right for taking such actions (Holtom & Burch, 2016). Other types of involuntary turnover include movement to different geographical locations, disability, retirement, and death (Bureau of Labor Statistics, 2016). Turnover affects productivity, safety, service quality, workplace efficiency, and team relationships in profits and nonprofits organizations (Li & Jones, 2013). A low turnover rate is crucial to business practices because of increased profits and sustainability (Haan, 2015; Jang & Kandampully, 2017). Pritchard (2014) suggested that 29% of new employees have the intention of resigning their jobs in the first year, which might indicate a gap and discrepancy between organizations' objectives and new hires' perceptions.

Employee retention in the education sector is a global problem with an annual turnover rate of 7.7%; 77 out of 1,000 full-time employees in the United States leave an organization for other opportunities (Bonenberger, Aikins, Akweongo, & Wyss, 2014). Because higher education employees must have appropriate credentials, the hiring process takes longer because of the delay involved in finding individuals with the appropriate qualifications to fill the vacancy (Punnoose & Ajit, 2016). Huang and Su (2016) noted that reducing employee turnover is essential to succeed in a global competitive marketplace.

Terera and Ngirande (2014) stated that leaders of educational institutions struggled managing employee turnover because of the lack of research on employee retention in the education sector. Additionally, other experts noted that leaders need to do more than reduce employee turnover by focusing their efforts on retaining top professionals (Musah & Nkuah, 2013; Qureshi & Wasti, 2014). An effective employee turnover reduction strategy must target the retention of top performance and employees with critical organizational skills.

Nonprofit leaders can decrease employee turnover by offering employees enhanced incentives, which leads to improved organizational commitment and lower employees' resistance to organizational changes (Musah & Nkuah, 2013; Neves, 2014). Because high turnover has a significant impact on organizations, educational leaders must implement strategies to increase employee retention (Terera & Ngirande, 2014). Leaders who are effective at reducing employee turnover, help organizations increase sustainability and productivity (George, 2015; Monteith, Burns, Rupp, & Mihalec-Adkins, 2016).

Effects of Employee Turnover in Nonprofit Education

The primary goal of educational leaders is to provide a learning environment where students can grow and get them ready for their professions upon graduation. In contrast, some higher education leaders continue to fail to prepare students for the workforce (Gitsham & Clark, 2014; Rodriguez, Green, Sun, & Baggerly-Hinojosa, 2017). Scholars found that increased employee turnover is one of the main reason colleges and universities are not properly preparing students for their careers (Gitsham & Clark, 2014; Rodriguez et al., 2017). Colleges and universities must provide students with high-quality education, and one way they can improve quality is by retaining experienced educators.

Instead of focusing on strategies to improve quality by retaining top employees, nonprofit higher education administrators are shifting their efforts to achieve other personal objectives (Gitsham & Clark, 2014). Leadership teams in the education sector mostly allocate organizational resources to increasing the financial status of their organizations. There is nothing wrong with caring about the financial well-being of one's organization, but leaders should not do so at the expense of quality. Elwick and Cannizzaro (2017) stated that some nonprofit leaders tend to compromise quality to achieve other goals. Using any approach that endangers the quality of the education students receive is unacceptable if the role of colleges and universities is to bring positive social change through high-quality education.

Education is a globally traded commodity worldwide. Therefore, educational leaders should take advantage of this trend bring positive social change (Altbach, 2015). Nonprofit administrators must find a balance between the financial performance of their organizations and fulfilling their responsibility of promoting positive social change (Elwick & Cannizzaro, 2017). Because poor-quality education can have a significant impact on the performance of our economy over time, higher education leaders should never compromise quality. The refractive thinker® approach provides valuable insight leaders can use to minimize the effects associated with employee turnover.

Increased employee turnover leads to a higher annual operational budget. Researchers found that organizational leaders who are not effective at reducing employee turnover had to larger operational budget as compared to competitors who had implanted effective employee retention strategies (Boykin, 2015; Naim & Lenka, 2017; Rajan, 2016). Azizova (2017) also found that ineffective employee turnover reduction strategies had a negative effect on the financial performance of nonprofit higher education, which led to fewer resources for leaders to allocate to other organizational objectives.

Approaches to Reduce Employee Turnover in Nonprofit Higher Education

Retaining employees is imperative because leaders who use effective employee retention strategies can avoid the costs associated with recruiting and replacing employees (George, 2015). Other costs related to increased employee turnover include reduced effectiveness in resource management (Musah & Nkuah, 2013; Rai & Lakshman, 2014). Nelissen, Forrier, and Verbruggen (2016) expressed that implementing effective business strategies managers can decrease employee turnover in educational institutions. Moreover, Mawanza (2017) suggested that reducing employee turnover benefits not only the organization, but also the employees because an increase in turnover leads to low productivity and higher levels of stress among workers. Researchers found that nonprofit educational leaders who implement effective strategies to reduce employee help their institutions gain a competitive advantage (Mawanza, 2017; Menon, 2014). Because nonprofit administrators in education have difficulty retaining employees, leaders must care about the establishment of employee turnover reduction strategies (George, 2015; Machin, 2014). The retention of critical employees is essential to the survival of any organization.

George (2015) noted many strategies nonprofit leaders could use to reduce employee turnover, but among the most effective strategies is providing employees with a safe operational environment. Machin (2014) added that safety is a vital human need most individuals require to be capable of effectively executing their duties at their workplace. Researchers found that workers who felt safe were more productive and committed to their organizations, as opposed to employees who felt unsafe (George, 2015; Machin, 2014). When employees work in an unsafe work environment, they perceive leaders do not care about them. Based on the findings of George (2015) and Machin (2014), creating a safe working environment is crucial to reducing employee turnover; by creating a safe environment, leaders gain a competitive advantage over competitors. Bush (2017) agreed that nonprofit administrators who are effective at retaining employees empower their organizations and promote a culture of increased productivity.

An effective training program can reduce the expensive associated with hiring external applicants since the organization will already have a large pool of qualified applicants. Promoting employees from within the company increases employees' loyalty and commitment to the organization, which leads to increased employee retention (Machin, 2014). Leaders who offer developmental training programs to their workers create an organization culture that promote employees' commitment, which in turn reduces employees' turnover intentions (Bush, 2017; Machin, 2014; Mamiseishvili, 2011).

Organizations with leaders who have daily interactions with employees and receive feedback have higher retention rates than institutions with leaders who did not communicate with workers on a regular basis (Patel & Hamlin, 2015). Lyons and Akroyd (2014) and Shahrill (2014) agreed that leaders who create an atmosphere that supports open communication were effective at increasing employees' job satisfaction. Based on the findings of Lyons and Akroyd (2014) and Patel and Hamlin (2015), effective communication between employees and leaders is an effective strategy to reduce employee turnover in the education sector.

Leadership Support in Nonprofit Higher Education

Scholars examined the connection between leadership support and its effects on employee retention and career success (Lu, Tu, Li, & Ho, 2016; Tymon, Stumpf, & Smith, 2011). Tymon et al. (2011) chose a sample of 9,301 participants and found that when leaders are supportive, and organizations have progressive opportunities, employees' perceptions of career success are more positive. Nonprofit leaders have a more significant role in retaining employees than reported in the literature (Tymon et al., 2011). Lu et al. (2016) also revealed that employees of organizations with supportive leaders had a positive perception of success, which led to a reduction in employee turnover intentions.

Supportive leaders can reduce workers' stress, which leads to a reduction in employees' turnover intentions. Lowering employees' stress levels is necessary because high stress results in employees' job dissatisfaction (Brenner et al., 2014; Herrmann & Felfe, 2014). When it comes to employees' stress, educational administrators face the same challenges as leaders in other sectors. Therefore, educational leaders need to support their team members as a strategy to reduce employee turnover (Khoiri, 2017). By offering staff continuous guidance and support, nonprofit leaders can reduce employees' stress (Buzeti, Klun, & Stare, 2016). Managers who recognize how to reduce employee stress are effective at decreasing employee turnover intentions (Thomas, Cornuel, & Harney, 2013).

Workers in nonprofit higher education appreciate leaders willing to prepare and mentor them for future opportunities in the organization (Naim & Lenka, 2017). Administrators who provide valuable mentorship to their subordinates are effective at decreasing employee turnover (Naim & Lenka, 2017; Lee & Mao, 2015). Leaders who spend time mentoring employees increase organizational commitment, which in turn increases productivity and reduces employee turnover (Ugoani, 2016; Yang & Zheng, 2015). Researchers found that nonprofit organizations that have leaders who mentored their followers had lower turnover rates (Azanza, Moriano, Molero, & Lévy Mangin, 2015; Smith & Nadelson, 2016; Ugoani, 2016). An effective mentorship program leads to increased employees' commitment and better organization performance (Rathi & Lee, 2015). In addition, leaders can use other recommendations found in the Refractive Thinker® series to support their employees and in turn reduce employee turnover.

Work-Life Balance Programs

Scholars recommended leaders stimulate work-life balance as a strategy to reduce employee turnover (Helmle, Botero, & Seibold, 2014; Lyons & Akroyd, 2014; Timms et al., 2014). Work-life balance refers to the balance between employees' jobs and their personal lives (Helmle et al., 2014). Individuals need work-life balance; a lack of work-life balance leads to excessive stress in a person's life (Timms et al., 2014; Valenzuela, Bellei, & Ríos, 2014). Employees who do not have a balance between family and work have increased stress, while employees who have an equilibrium between their jobs and families have reduced stress (Timms et al., 2014). A lack of work-life balance is precarious for most professionals because of the time-consuming of handling employment requirements and meeting families' expectations. Work and family are important for many employees, they should not have to choose one over the other. A lack of balance between work and family leads to conflict. Researchers found that conflict leads to fatigue and increase employee turnover (Thacker, 2015; Timms et al., 2014). By providing employees of nonprofit colleges or universities with work-life balance such as work-from-home options and flex time, nonprofit leaders can reduce employee turnover (Jaiswal & Dhar, 2016; Lyons & Akroyd, 2014).

Leaders should offer flexible work schedules when necessary to help employees have a balance between job requirements and personal life (George, 2015; Sweet, Pitt-Catsouphes, & James, 2017). Some educational leaders are hesitant to recognize that work-life balance influences employee turnover (Deery & Jago, 2015; Terera & Ngirande, 2014). Failing to provide employees with flexible work schedules leads to increased stress and conflicts. Nawaz and Pangil (2016) and Trefalt (2013) stated that employees continue to have difficulty balancing time between home and work. Trefalt found a lack of work-life balance can lead to problems such as increased stress, divorce, depression, and substance abuse. Work stress leads to increased employee' job dissatisfaction and reduced productivity, which in turn increases employee turnover intentions (Lyons & Akroyd, 2014; Trepanier, Fernet, & Austin, 2016).

Although some workers can manage an unbalanced life, most individuals would be severely affected over time (Chatrakul Na Ayudhya, Prouska, & Lewis, 2015; Farivar, Cameron, & Yaghoubi, 2016; Lawson, Davis, Crouter, & O'Neill, (2013). Lawson et al. (2013) found that work-life balance is a predictor of turnover among employees. Improving employees' work-life balance also decreases leaders' stress as the result of fewer employees' absences and reduce employee turnover (de Sivatte, Gordon, Rojo, & Olmos, 2015; Lawson et al., 2013). When implementing an effective employee turnover reducing strategy, leaders need to consider the effects of employees' work-life balance.

Presentation of the Findings

To collect data on effective strategies nonprofit higher education leaders use to reduce employee turnover, La Salle (2018) conducted 10 interviews with leaders at a nonprofit college. La Salle (2018) and Beato (2017) used semistructured interviews with open-ended questions to allow participants to answer the interview questions on strategies they used to reduce employee turnover and maintain sustainability. By using open-ended questions, participants were able to share their experiences without the restrictions of quantitative data collection methods. La Salle and Beato also reviewed company documents on employee turnover including memorandums and flyers.

Theme 1: Effective Communication Reduced Employee Turnover

Effective communication reduced employee turnover emerged from a thorough analysis of the participants' responses and organizational documents on employee turnover. Communication between leaders and employees is an effective strategy that leads to increased employee retention and engagement (P1, P2, P3, P4, and P5). Effective communication is a two-way process both leaders and employees use to exchange information. According to participants, leaders who communicate effectively increase job satisfaction, which in turn leads to reduced employee turnover and improved business practices (P4 and P5). P5 stated that he reduced employee turnover in his department from six to one from 2015 to 2017 by practicing effective communication with his team members. The data from the interviews indicated that leaders who practice effective communication are more effective at improving employee engagement and reducing employee turnover.

Another key element of effective communication is timely and consistent communication. By communicating with employees in a timely and consistent manner, leaders can reduce employee turnover intentions. According to Participant 4, leaders who communicate with their team members in a timely and consistent manner create an operational environment where workers are happier and less likely to leave. By providing followers with timely and consistent communication leaders can keep workers informed and reduce employee turnover (P4). Other participants shared that engaging in timely and consistent communication is an inexpensive way for leaders to improve retention (P1, P2, and P3). According to P2, leaders who communicate with their team members consistently are more effective at reducing turnover than leaders who do not. Being consistent and knowing when the time is right to engage in a two-way conversation with workers is an effective strategy to reduce employee turnover. By communicating with employees on a consistent basis, leaders can identify and address issues that are affecting employees' satisfaction, which leads to a decrease of employees' dissatisfaction and employee turnover. Based on the participants' responses, memorandums, and organizational policy letters, La Salle (2018) and Beato (2017) reviewed while conducting this research, leaders can reduce employee turnover intentions by communicating in a consistent and timely manner with their followers.

Participants shared that honest communication is an integral part of effective communication. To reduce employee turnover, leaders must be honest when communicating with their employees (P1 and P3). According to P4, being honest with employees reduces employee turnover because honest communication increases organizational commitment. Committed employees are less likely to seek for other employment opportunities as opposed to workers not committed to their jobs. Leaders who practice open and honest communication are more effective at building healthy relationships with employees than leaders who are dishonest or simply hide some information from subordinates (P2 and P4). Employees appreciate honesty, even when leaders give unsatisfactory news (P4). Lack of honest communication from leaders fosters distrust among employees, which leads to increased job dissatisfaction and reduced employee retention (Wiley, 2017). Open and honest communication promotes a sense of trust and strengthens cooperation between leaders and employees, which in turn fosters job satisfaction and reduces employee turnover.

P3 and P5 commented that the lack of communication from employees or leaders has an adverse effect on leaders' efforts to reduce employee turnover and leads to lack of cooperation and trust among leaders and employees. Leaders who create a work environment that promotes effective information flow earn the trust of their employees; increased trust leads to improved retention (P2, P6, and P10). Conversely, leaders who do not communicate effectively with their employees increase job dissatisfaction and turnover intentions because of lack of trust and cooperation. One of the benefits of effective communication is that it creates an operating environment that leads to improved employee cooperation, increased participation, and enhanced trust. When workers trust their leaders, employees are more willing to participate in their organizations' decision-making process, which increases loyalty, productivity, job satisfaction, and commitment. An increase in loyalty leads to increased commitment and loyalty, which reduces employee turnover intentions. By creating an operating environment based on trust and collaboration, leaders can increase employee satisfaction, which benefits both the employees and the organization.

Theme 2: Creating a Supportive Work Environment Reduced Employee Turnover

Creating a supportive work environment is another strategy leaders can use to reduce employee turnover. By creating a supportive work environment, leaders can create a healthy work environment where workers are happier, which leads to a reduction of employee turnover intention (P4 and P5). Leaders who create a supportive work environment improve the relationship between leaders and employees; which in turn reduces employee turnover (P2).

A supportive work environment occurs when leaders are available for their followers during the good times and bad times (P3 and P10). A supportive work environment promotes team cohesion and collaboration. An increase in collaboration has a positive effect on productivity and performance. Leaders who support their team members can increase productivity and employee performance (P2, P5, and P9). The analysis of participant responses revealed that leaders who create a supportive work environment are effective at reducing employee turnover.

One of the benefits of a supportive work environment is an improvement in leader-subordinate relationship; which in turn reduces employee turnover (P1, P2, and P4). By creating a supportive work environment P3 reported that he reduced employed turnover from 20% in 2016 to 7% in 2017. La Salle (2018) asked participants how many employees were in their department; P3 said, "We have 30 employees; my department had six turnovers in 2016 and only 2 in 2017." Six turnovers in P3's department with 30 employees equal a 20% turnover in 2016; two turnovers in 2017 represents a 7% turnover for the department. The data shared by P3 revealed a 13% reduction on employee turnover from 2016 to 2017.

Numerous participants mentioned that they use supportive leadership as a strategy to reduce employee turnover (P1, P2, P3, P4, P6, P8, and P10). According to some particpants, supportive leaders are more effective at decreasing employee turnover than leaders who do not set time aside to find ways to support their team members (P1 and P4). P1 shared that in the last 3 years there has been a significant increase of supportive leaders at this organization. According to P1, using a supportive leadership strategy is responsible for a decrease in employee turnover at this organization. P3 supported the comment made by of P1 by confirming that leaders leaders who support their team members create a supportive work environment that leads to a reduction of employee turnover. The comments from participants revealed that at this organization supportive leadership led to a healthy work environment, which in turn reduced employee turnover intentions.

Theme 3: Job Satisfaction Decreased Turnover

La Salle (2018) and Beato (2017) reviewed organizational documents including memorandums on employee turnover and organizational policy letters. Our goal for reviewing organizational document was to triangulate the data from the interviews with the data collected from the documents. By using two sources of data collection (interviews and organizational documents), La Salle and Beato were able to validate the data used for the data analysis. An employee turnover memorandum from 2016 had the following information, "Promoting job satisfaction is the best way our leaders can help us reduce employee turnover." We read a policy letter from the college president published in 2017 stating that department leaders must implement a strategy that leads to improved job satisfaction for our employee. Based on the information collected from organizational documents; leaders might reduce employee turnover by communicating with their employees through memorandums, and policy letters.

Some participants emphasized that to reduce employee turnover leaders should consentrate on increasing employees' job satisfaction (P1, P2, P3, P4, P7, and P9). Job dissatisfaction is one of the primary causes of increased employee turnover intentions. Participants also commented that leaders who promote job satisfaction are effective at reducing employee turnover intentions (P1, P4, P5, and P10). To effectively reduce employee turnover, educational leaders need to invest more time talking to employees to measure their levels of job satisfaction. The data analysis of participants' responses indicated that increased job satisfaction leads to a decrease in employee turnover. Other participants (P1, P3, and P4) noted that compensation reduces employee turnover intentions. P3 shared that the main reason workers leave their jobs is to go work for another university with better compensation. Although most professors love teaching, they also expect adequate compensation to support their families (P2 and P5). According to P4, employees who find jobs at other universities are often the best qualified to teach. Based on the data analysis of participants' responses, leaders can reduce employee turnover by increasing job satisfaction and offering employees competitive compensation.

Job satisfaction refers to the workers' attitudes about their jobs (Drydakis, 2015). Several participants stated that by increasing employee job satisfaction, leaders can reduce employee turnover (P1, P2, P4, P5, P7, and P8). P2 stated that strategic leaders can increase employees' job satisfaction by setting time aside to communicate with employees to measure their level of job satisfaction. By understanding employees' job satisfaction leaders can reduce employee turnover intentions. Employees' job satisfaction should not be overlooked because unhappy workers have negative attitude toward their job. Employees' attitude leads to reduced productivity, lower customer satisfaction, and increased employee turnover. Conversely, employees with a high level of job satisfaction perform better and contribute to the achievement of the organization's goal. Based on participants' responses and organizational documents, nonprofit higher education leaders can reduce employee turnover by promoting job satisfaction.

Conclusion

Based on the data gathered from the literature, participant responses, and organizational documents on employee turnover, nonprofit higher education leaders can reduce employee turnover by communicating effectively with their employees, creating a supportive work environment, and increasing employee job satisfaction. By using the strategies shared by participants, nonprofit higher education leaders can also promote organizational commitment, increase employees' loyalty, and encourage teamwork and cooperation among employees in their organizations. Creating an operational environment that increases employee retention has a positive effect in the performance and productivity of healthcare organizations. In addition, implementing strategies focused on the retention of top performers lead to increased organizational commitment and engagement. Another factor leaders need to consider is that the strategies participant recommended are less expensive than the costs associated with hiring new qualified employees. La Salle (2018) and Beato (2017) recommend that nonprofit higher education leaders, scholars, and practitioners use the recommendations participant shared to gain new insight on the employee turnover reduction strategies that other leaders found effective at other nonprofit higher education institutions. In addition, higher education leaders who can use a refractive thinking approach in their strategies to reduce employee turnover might create an operational environment that leads to long-term success in their organizations.

THOUGHTS FROM THE ACADEMIC ENTREPRENEUR

The problem to be solved:

- Reducing employee turnover in nonprofit higher education
- Strategies for leaders to reduce employee turnover

The goals:

- Provide leaders with effectively strategies to reduce employee turnover
- Share insights that can lead to increased awareness of employee turnover

The questions to ask:

- Are leaders using effective strategies to increase employee retention?
- How can effective employee turnover reduction strategies save my organization money?
- Is my organization's employee retention strategy effective?
- What are the long-term effects of an increase in employee turnover?

Today's Business Application:

- By understanding strategies used by leaders to reduce employee turnover in the higher education sector, other leaders can increase productivity and profitability and promote organizational growth.
- Leaders must dedicate organizational resources towards the retention of top performers.
- Leaders who care about the retention of top performers increase organizational productivity and performance, which in turn promotes increased sustainability and growth.

REFERENCES

Altbach, P. (2015). Knowledge and education as international commodities. *International Higher Education, 28*, 2-5. doi:10.6017/ihe.2002.28.6657

Azanza, G., Moriano, J. A., Molero, F., & Lévy Mangin, J. P. (2015). The effects of authentic leadership on turnover intention. *Leadership & Organization Development Journal, 36*, 955-971. doi:10.1108/LODJ-03-2014-0056

Azizova, Z. T. (2017). Closing the opportunity gap: Identity-conscious strategies for retention and student success ed. by Vijay Pendakur. *The Review of Higher Education, 40*, 623-627. doi:10.1353/rhe.2017.0025

Bandura, R., & R. Lyons, P. (2014). Short-term fixes fall short when it comes to keeping the best employees: Successful firms invest time, money and commitment in retention. *Human Resource Management International Digest, 22*(5), 29-32. doi:10.1108/HRMID-07-2014-0101

Beato, A. (2017). *Effective strategies employed by retail store leaders to reduce employee turnover* (Doctoral dissertation). Retrieved from ProQuest Dissertations & Theses Global. (Order No. 10278363)

Belke, A., & Keil, J. (2016). Financial integration, global liquidity and global macroeconomic linkages. *Journal of Economic Studies, 43*(1), 16-26. doi:10.1108/jes-02-2015-0026

Bonenberger, M., Aikins, M., Akweongo, P., & Wyss, K. (2014). The effects of health worker motivation and job satisfaction on turnover intention in Ghana: A cross-sectional study. *Human Resources Health, 12*(1), 12-43. doi:10.1186/1478-4491-12-43

Boykin, T. F. (2015). For profit, for success, for black men: A review of literature on urban for-profit colleges and universities. *Urban Education, 52*, 1140-1162. doi:10.1177/0042085915618724

Brenner, M. H., Andreeva, E., Theorell, T., Goldberg, M., Westerlund, H., Leineweber, C., & Bonnaud, S. (2014). Organizational downsizing and depressive symptoms in the European recession: The experience of workers in France, Hungary, Sweden and the United Kingdom. *PLoS ONE, 9*(5), 1-14. doi10.1371/journal.pone.0097063

Bureau of Labor Statistics. (2015). Job openings and labor turnover survey news release. Retrieved from http://www.bls.gov/news.release/jolts.htm

Bureau of Labor Statistics. (2016). Job openings and labor turnover survey news release. Retrieved from http://www.bls.gov/news.release/jolts.nr0.htm

Bush, T. (2017). The enduring power of transformational leadership. *Educational Management Administration & Leadership, 45*, 563-565. doi:10.1177/1741143217701827

Buzeti, J., Klun, M., & Stare, J. (2016). Evaluation of measures to reduce employee turnover in Slovenian organizations. *E&M Ekonomie a Management, 19*(1), 121-131. doi:10.15240/tul/001/2016-1-009

Chahal, H., & Bakshi, P. (2015). Examining intellectual capital and competitive advantage relationship: Role of innovation and organizational learning. *International Journal of Bank Marketing, 33,* 376-399. doi:10.1108/IJBM-07-2013-0069

Chatrakul Na Ayudhya, U., Prouska, R., & Lewis, S. (2015). Work-life balance can benefit business during financial crisis and austerity: Human resources (HR) must convince management of the need for a flexible approach. *Human Resource Management International Digest, 23*(5), 25-28. doi:10.1108/HRMID-05-2015-0078

de Sivatte, I., Gordon, J., Rojo, P., & Olmos, R. (2015). The impact of work-life culture on organizational productivity. *Personnel Review, 44,* 883-905. doi:10.1108/PR 12-2013-0226

Deery, M., & Jago, L. (2015). Revisiting talent management, work-life balance and retention strategies. *International Journal of Contemporary Hospitality Management, 27,* 453-472. doi:10.1108/IJCHM-12-2013-0538

Drydakis, N. (2015). Effect of sexual orientation on job satisfaction: Evidence from Greece. Industrial Relations: *A Journal of Economy and Society, 54*(1), 162-187.

Ekdale, B., Tully, M., Harmsen, S., & Singer, J. B. (2015). Newswork within a culture of job insecurity: Producing news amidst organizational and industry uncertainty. *Journalism Practice, 9,* 383-398. doi:10.1080/17512786.2014.963376

Elwick, A., & Cannizzaro, S. (2017). Happiness in higher education. *Higher Education Quarterly, 71,* 204-219. doi:10.1111/hequ.12121

Farivar, F., Cameron, R., & Yaghoubi, M. (2016). Work-family balance and cultural dimensions: From a developing nation perspective. *Personnel Review, 45,* 315-333. doi:10.1108/PR-09-2014-0196

George, C. (2015). Retaining professional workers: What makes them stay? *Employee Relations, 37*(1), 102-121. doi:10.1108/ER-10-2013-0151

Gitsham, M., & Clark, T. (2014). Market demand for sustainability in management education. *International Journal of Sustainability in Higher Education, 15*(3), 291-303. doi:10.1108/IJSHE-12-2011-0082

Haan, H. (2015). Competitive advantage, what does it really mean in the context of public higher education institutions? *International Journal of Educational Management, 29*(1), 44-61. doi:10.1108/IJEM-07-2013-0115

Helmle, J., Botero, I., & Seibold, D. (2014). Factors that influence perceptions of work-life balance in owners of copreneurial firms. *Journal of Family Business Management, 4*(2), 110-132. doi:10.1108/JFBM-06-2014-0013

Herrmann, D., & Felfe, J. (2014). Effects of leadership style, creativity technique and personal initiative on employee creativity. *British Journal of Management, 25*(2), 209-227. doi:10.1111/j.1467-8551.2012.00849

Holtom, B., & Burch, T. (2016). A model of turnover-based disruption in customer services. *Human Resource Management Review, 26*(1), 25-36. doi:10.1016/j.hrmr.2015.09.004

Huang, W., & Su, C. (2016). The mediating role of job satisfaction in the relationship between job training satisfaction and turnover intentions. *Industrial and Commercial Training, 48*(1), 42-52. doi:10.1108/ICT-04-2015

Jaiswal, D., & Dhar, R. L. (2016). Impact of perceived organizational support, psychological empowerment and leader member exchange on commitment and its subsequent impact on service quality. *International Journal of Productivity and Performance Management, 65*(1), 58-79. doi:10.1108/IJPPM-03-2014-0043

Jang, J., & Kandampully, J. (2017). Reducing employee turnover intention through servant leadership in the restaurant context: A mediation study of affective organizational commitment. *International Journal of Hospitality &Tourism Administration, 2017*, 1-17. doi:10.1080/15256480.2017.1305310

Khoiri, N. (2017). Madrasah culture based transformational leadership model. *Nadwa, 10*(2), 151-156. doi:10.21580/nw.2016.10.2.1160

La Salle, D. J. (2018). *Strategies for profit educational leaders use to reduce employee turnover and maintain sustainability* (unpublished doctoral dissertation). Walden University, Minneapolis, MN.

Lawson, K., Davis, K., Crouter, A., & O'Neill, J. (2013). Understanding work-family spillover in hotel managers. *International Journal of Hospitality Management, 33*, 273-281. doi:10.1016/j.ijhm.2012.09.003

Lee, Y., & Mao, P. (2015). Survivors of organizational change: A resource perspective. *Business and Management Studies, 1*(2), 1-5. doi:10.11114/bms.v1i2.692

Li, Y., & Jones, C. (2013). A literature review of nursing turnover costs. *Journal of Nursing Management, 21*, 405-418. doi:10.1111/j.1365-2834.2012.01411.x

Lu, X., Tu, Y., Li, Y., & Ho, C. C. (2016). Affective and normative forces between HCHRM and turnover intention in China. *Employee Relations, 38*, 741-754. doi:10.1108/er-09-2015-0181

Lyons, F., & Akroyd, D. (2014). The impact of human capital and selected job rewards on community college faculty job satisfaction. *Community College Journal of Research and Practice, 38*, 194-207. doi:10.1080/10668926.2014.851965

Machin, D. (2014). Professional educator or professional manager? The contested role of the for-profit international school principal. *Journal of Research in International Education, 13*(1), 19-29. doi:10.1177/1475240914521347

Mamiseishvili, K. (2011). Characteristics, job satisfaction, and workplace perceptions of foreign-born faculty at public 2-year institutions. *Community College Review, 39*(1), 26-45. doi:10.1177/0091552110394650

Mawanza, W. (2017). The effects of stress on employee productivity: A perspective of Zimbabwe's socio-economic dynamics of 2016. *Journal of Economics and Behavioral Studies, 9*(2), 22-27. doi:10.22610/jebs.v9i2.1647

Menon, M. (2014). The relationship between transformational leadership, perceived leader effectiveness and teachers' job satisfaction. *Journal of Educational Administration, 52*, 509-528. doi:10.1108/jea-01-2013-0014

Mok, K. H. (2014). Enhancing quality of higher education for world-class status: Approaches, strategies, and challenges for Hong Kong. *Chinese Education & Society, 47*(1), 44-64. doi:10.2753/CED1061-1932470103

Monteith, M., Burns, M., Rupp, D., & Mihalec-Adkins, B. (2016). Out of work and out of luck? Layoffs, system justification, and hiring decisions for people who have been laid off. *Social Psychological and Personality Science, 7*(1), 77-84. doi:10.1177/1948550615599827

Musah, A., & Nkuah, J. (2013). Reducing employee turnover in tertiary institutions in Ghana: The role of motivation. *Journal of Education and Practice, 4*(18), 115-134. Retrieved from https://iiste.org/Journals/index.php/JEP

Naim, M. F., & Lenka, U. (2017). How does mentoring contribute to Gen Y employees' intention to stay? An Indian perspective. *Europe's Journal of Psychology, 13*, 314-335. doi:10.5964/ejop.v13i2.1304

Nawaz, M., & Pangil, F. (2016). The relationship between human resource development factors, career growth and turnover intention: The mediating role of organizational commitment. *Management Science Letters, 6*(2), 157-176. doi:10.5267/j.msl.2015.12.006

Nelissen, J., Forrier, A., & Verbruggen, M. (2016). Employee development and voluntary turnover: Testing the employability paradox. *Human Resource Management Journal, 27*(1), 152-168. doi:10.1111/1748-8583.12136

Neves, P. (2014). Taking it out on survivors: Submissive employees, downsizing, and abusive supervision. *Journal of Occupational and Organizational Psychology, 87*, 507-534. doi:10.1111/joop.12061

Patel, T., & Hamlin, R. (2015). Toward a unified framework of perceived negative leader behaviors insights from French and British educational sectors. *Journal of Business Ethics, 12*(1), 1-26. doi:10.1007/s10551-015-2909-5

Pritchard, K. (2014). Using employee surveys to attract and retain the best talent. *Strategic HR Review, 13*(2), 59-62. doi:10.1108/SHR-10-2013-0100

Punnoose, R., & Ajit, P. (2016). Prediction of employee turnover in organizations using machine learning algorithms. *International Journal of Advanced Research in Artificial Intelligence, 5*, 590-594. doi:10.14569/ijarai.2016.0509040029

Qureshi, M., & Wasti, S. (2014). Lay-off survivor sickness syndrome: Investigating the lasting impact on performance of survivors in the context of age and gender in private sector organizations of Pakistan. *International Journal of Human Resource Studies, 4*(3), 178-197. doi:10.5296/ijhrs.v4i3.6078

Rai, S., & Lakshman, C. (2014). Organizational culture and commitment among lay-off survivors: A tale of two MNCs in India. *South Asian Journal of Management, 21*(4), 1-21. Retrieved from http://www.sajm-amdisa.org/

Rajan, D. (2016). Employee turnover and employee performance: A study among nurses. *Anveshak International Journal of Management, 5*(2), 121-129. doi:10.15410/aijm/2016/v5i2/100694

Ramlall, S., Al-Sabaan, S., & Magbool, S. (2014). Layoffs, coping, and commitment: Impact of layoffs on employees and strategies used in coping with layoffs. *International Journal of Management and Strategy, 5*(2), 25-30. doi:10.5430/jms.v5n2p25

Rathi, N., & Lee, K. (2015). Retaining talent by enhancing organizational prestige: An HRM strategy for employees working in the retail sector. *Personnel Review, 44*(4), 142-149. doi:10.1108/PR-05-2013-007

Rodriguez, R. A., Green, M. T., Sun, Y., & Baggerly-Hinojosa, B. (2017). Authentic leadership and transformational leadership: An incremental approach. *Journal of Leadership Studies, 11*(1), 20-35. doi:10.1002/jls.21501

Samuel, M. O., & Chipunza, C. (2013). Attrition and retention of senior academics at institutions of higher learning in South Africa: The strategies, complexities and realities. *Journal of Social Sciences, 35*(2), 97-109. doi:10.1080/09718923.2013.11893151

Selesho, J. M., & Naile, I. (2014). Academic staff retention as a human resource factor: University perspective. *The International Business & Economics Research Journal (Online), 13*(2), 295-304. doi:10.19030/iber.v13i2.8444

Shahrill, M. (2014). Exploring educational administration: The relationship between leadership and management. *International Journal of Academic Research in Business and Social Sciences, 4*, 525-538. doi:10.1080./08941920.2013.861561

Smith, J., & Nadelson, L. (2016). Learning for you and learning for me: Mentoring professional development for mentor teachers. *Mentoring & Tutoring: Partnership in Learning, 24*(1), 59-72. doi:10.1080/13611267.2016.1165489

Sun, R., & Wang, W. (2016). Transformational leadership, employee turnover intention, and actual voluntary turnover in public organizations. *Public Management Review, 19*, 1124-1141. doi:10.1080/14719037.2016.1257063

Sweet, S., Pitt-Catsouphes, M., & James, J. B. (2017). Manager attitudes concerning flexible work arrangements: Fixed or changeable? *Community, Work & Family, 20*(1), 50-71. doi:10.1080/13668803.2016.1271311

Terera, S., & Ngirande, H. (2014). The impact of training on employee job satisfaction and retention among administrative staff members: A case of a selected tertiary institution. *Journal Social Science, 39*(1), 43-50. doi:10.1080/09718923.2014.11893267

Thacker, R. (2015). The application of social exchange to commitment bonds of pro-union employees: Cognitive calculations of reciprocity. *Human Resource Management Review, 25*(3), 287-297. doi:10.1016/j.hrmr.2014.10.001

Thomas, H., Cornuel, E., & Harney, S. (2013). Management education: Unfulfilled promises and new prospects. *Journal of Management Development, 32*, 560-566. doi:10.1108/jmd.2013.02632eaa.001

Timms, C., Brough, P., O'Driscoll, M., Kalliath, T., Siu, O. L., Sit, C., & Lo, D. (2014). Flexible work arrangements, work engagement, turnover intentions and psychological health. *Asia Pacific Journal of Human Resources, 53*(1), 83-103. doi:10.1111/1744-7941.12030

Trefalt, S. (2013). Between you and me: Setting work-nonwork boundaries in the context of workplace relationships. *Academy of Management Journal, 56*, 1802-1829. doi:10.5465/amj.2011.0298

Trepanier, S. G., Fernet, C., & Austin, S. (2016). Longitudinal relationships between workplace bullying, basic psychological needs, and employee functioning: Asimultaneous investigation of psychological need satisfaction and frustration. *European Journal of Work and Organizational Psychology, 25*, 690-706. doi:10.1080/1359432X.2015.1132200

Tschoop, C., Grote, G., & Gerber, M. (2014). How career orientation shapes the job satisfaction-turnover intention link. *Journal of Organizational Behavior, 35*(2), 151-171. doi:10.102/job.1857

Tymon W. G., Jr., Stumpf, S. A., & Smith, R. R. (2011). Manager support predicts turnover of professionals in India. *Career Development International, 16*(3), 293-312. doi:10.1108/13620431111140134

Ugoani, J. N. N. (2016). Employee turnover and productivity among small business entities in Nigeria. *Independent Journal of Management & Production, 7*, 1063-1082. doi:10.14807/ijmp.v7i4.466

Wiley, E. (2017). Cause and effective communication. *Chance, 30*(2), 30-37. doi:10.1080/09332480.2017.1320476

Yahaya, R., & Ebrahim, F. (2016). Leadership styles and organizational commitment: Literature review. *Journal of Management Development, 35*(2), 190-216. doi:10.1108/JMD-01-2015-0004

Yang, S., & Zheng, L. (2015). Perceived job insecurity of white and black workers: An expanded gap in organizations with layoff prevention commitment. *Sociological Spectrum, 35*, 483-503. doi:10.1080/02732173.2015.1064797

Valenzuela, J., Bellei, C., & Ríos, D. (2014). Socioeconomic school segregation in a market-oriented educational system: The case of Chile. *Journal of Education Policy, 29*(2), 217-241. doi:10.1080/02680939.2013.806995

About the Authors...

Dr. Denise J. La Salle resides in Orlando, Florida with her husband. She has three boys and two grandchildren. Dr. Denise is currently an adjunct professor at National University College. Currently, she owns and manages a used tires retail shop. Also, she opened three nonprofits which are La Salle Educational Foundation, International Books of Hope, and Adopt a Teacher Foundation. Her vision is to open schools in foreign countries for less privileged people. Dr. Denise is in the process of opening the first bilingual school and library in Bolivia. Her philosophy is *"I cannot change the world, but I can change the world of someone through education."*

Dr. Denise received a Doctor of Business Administration (DBA) in International Business from Walden University in 2018. A Master in Educational Leadership from Ana G. Mendez University in 2010 and a Bachelors in Elementary Education from Interamerican University of Puerto Rico. Recognized as a STAR teacher for excellence teaching, for which she became among the top 25% best teachers in Orange County, Florida. Dr. Denise received a recognition letter from the President of the United States in 2007. In her time off, she enjoys spending time with her grandchildren and traveling with her husband.

She has published two journal publications: La Salle, D. (2018). *Strategies for profit educational leaders use to reduce employee turnover and maintain sustainability* (Doctoral dissertation). Available from ProQuest

La Salle, D., Beato, A., & Velkova, G. (2018). Successful strategies used by leaders to reduce employee turnover and maintain sustainability in for-profit colleges. *The International Journal of Business & Management*. Retrieved from http://www.theijbm.com

To reach Dr. Denise J. La Salle for information, please contact her by **email: denisela08@yahoo.com**

 Dr. Alexandro Beato resides in El Paso, Texas with his wife and three children. Dr. Alexandro is currently an adjunct professor at Park University. He retired from the U.S. Army in 2015. Dr. Beato received a Doctor of Business Administration (DBA) in healthcare management from Walden University in 2017 and a Master of Business Administration (MBA) in marketing from Columbia Southern University in 2011. He also completed a master certificate in Lean Six Sigma from Villanova University in 2018. Dr. Alexandro also serves as a senior dissertation editor for Editors Dissertations and Thesis. In his time off, he enjoys mentoring and coaching students with their dissertations and helping them achieve their educational goals. He is passionate about researching organizational leadership, employee turnover, corporate performance, and employee retention.

Dr. Alexandro is also an active member of Delta Mu Delta Honor Society and Golden Key International Honor Society.

Dr. Alexandro is a best-selling author. He previously wrote a chapter on understanding employee turnover in the healthcare industry in *The Refractive Thinker®: Vol XIV: Healthcare: The Impact on Leadership, Business, and Education*. He has published two journal publications: *Implementing Effective Strategies to Reduce Employee Turnover: Retail Managers Share Experiences* and *Successful Strategies Leaders Use to Reduce Employee Turnover and Maintain Sustainability in For-Profit Colleges*. Additional work includes his dissertation: *Effective Strategies Employed by Retail Store Leaders to Reduce Employee Turnover*.

To reach Dr. Alexandro Beato, please contact him by **email: alexbeato1@yahoo.com**

CHAPTER 7

Development: A Praxis for Constructive Management and Dynamic Leadership

Dr. Evelyn Hollis

> Attitudes of leading and or managing are outmoded and may lack consideration of diversity, technology transference, knowledge management and generational differences.
> —Dr. Evelyn Hollis

How does one overcome an adversary or win over your competition in an environment of complexity and ambiguity? How does one lead when one's team or department encounters varied challenges and potential life-changing events? How does one deal with a funding cut from the government or review a program for effectiveness with the board? How does one deal with a talented member of staff that leaves? Disruptive, changing, hostile, along with multiplexed are characterizations of environments faced by civilian and military organizations. Development whether in the profit or the nonprofit sector, all organizations need managers and leaders with skills to successfully execute strategy. Responding to these challenges, requires managers and leaders to demonstrate a wide range of behaviors. Managers and leaders need to have a repertoire of knowledge and skills, and know when to apply those skills, as the situation dictates. Demands placed upon leaders fluctuate, as concerns of a leader's ability to resolve challenges are important to the organization. Leaders and managers must think, exercise judgement, and make proper decisions to meet those challenges. Strategic leaders and managers buy in or support for developmental initiatives must permeate throughout the organization to influence engagement and motivation towards enhancing or building upon skills.

The aim of this chapter is to distinguish variables within the development environment from the perspective of the organizational leader to develop skills that enable both managers and leaders to succeed in ever-changing conditions. Social and cultural perspectives, as well as dogma, influence the development environment and the strategies for developing managers and leaders with a specific skill set. Upwards of 2500 companies and personnel leaders in 94 countries around the world reported organizational aims to promote leader development and capabilities at all levels (Deloitte Consulting LLP and Bersin by Deloitte, 2014). The objective is to understand elements within the organization that enhance and or distract from development as well as the initiatives that offer the most success for developing human capital in an organization. The background from which the military began an appraisal of leader development offers insight into the similarities to discern the state of development for both profit and nonprofit organizations. The Refractive Thinker® proffers that rather than focusing on the differences of managers and leaders, consider both need a common capacity and that is to influence. To influence, one must be self –aware developing capacity for self-awareness requires recognition that there are variables in the environment that enhance or detract from growth. Managers and leaders who have the ability to be flexible, adaptive, and agile achieve success.

Background

Whether the operational environment or the organizational environment, managers and leaders need skills of flexibility, adaptability, and agility. The operating environment is the combination of circumstances and influences within which leaders and soldiers performs. The organizational environment is the combination of businesses and other forces that affect an organizations execution and advantages (Bateman, Snell, & Konopaske, 2017).

Operational environment. The increased operational tempo leaders work in created a need for leaders to know more and have a certain versatility and capability. Adaptable leaders, culturally proficient, flexible, and agile ready to face the demands of the environment (Vane, 2011). There was a need to understand the state of leader development. The Training and Doctrine Command (TRADOC) formed an officer, noncommissioned officer (NCO) and warrant officer Army Training Leader Development Panel (ATLDP) to gauge the condition of development as leaders at all levels continued to see an increase in challenges and complexity (Headquarters, Department of the Army, 2000). Panel findings produced several implications for leader development. Acknowledging that, since 1990, strategic leaders recognized a need to change training and leader development programs to still be relevant to the contemporary operating environment and that current programs were not effective (Headquarters, Department of the Army, 2000). Additionally, suggesting a need for skills of flexibility, adaptability, and agility for current and future leaders (Headquarters, Department of the Army, 2002).

Organizational environment. Consider that managers and leaders in nonprofit organizations might face vague, conflicting missions, and or reduced resources requiring the skills and ability to manage complex situations. For-profit organizations require managers and leaders who have not only the knowledge and skill to identify strategies to achieve financial goals and initiate new activities but also to create innovations to bring about even greater profits (Kahnweiler, 2013; Rojas, 2000). Non-profits need to forecast for the future and operate like a business yet not forget their purpose (Kahnweiler,

2013). The similarities continue between profit, nonprofits and military organizations in levels of leading and levels of functions.

Levels of leading. Military organizations associate specific responsibilities to strategic, organizational and direct level leader. Profit and nonprofit organizations associate specific responsibilities to the top-level, mid-level and front-line managers. Strategic leaders deliver the vision and top-level managers are responsible for the organization's overall management. The organizational leader composes the framework, processes, and systems that bring together the vision and direct objectives. Mid-level managers explain and interpret goals and plans into specific objectives and activities. Direct leaders have face-to-face contact just as the front-line manager supervises operations within the organization. Managers and leaders at all levels must have the capacity to create desired effects through their knowledge and their skills.

Levels of function. Military organizations associate specific skills and abilities to strategic, organizational and tactical levels of conflict. This relationship reinforces leaders having the capacity to create desired effects through their knowledge. Manager skills within the process of designing, arranging, influencing, and executing parallel knowledge and abilities at the strategic, tactical and operational level. The levels are hierarchical in nature; however, environments are increasingly complex, requiring managers at all levels to interact, create, and innovate (Bateman, Snell, & Konopaske, 2017).

Manager and leader. The senior NCOs' role and level of responsibility in a military organization is commensurate with the role and level of responsibility of managers in civilian profit and nonprofit sectors (Hollis, 2017; Joiner & Josephs, 2007). The population surveyed to appraise the state of development in the military consisted of mid and junior officers and NCOs working at the direct position of leadership additionally, a smaller number of officers and

NCOs working at strategic and organizational positions (Headquarters, Department of the Army, 2002). A finding from the assessment of leader development revealed potential performance gaps in skill growth from an organizational level (Headquarters, Department of the Army, 2002). A focus of the case study was to understand development from the perspective of senior NCOs operating and working at the organizational level (Hollis, 2017). A refractive thinking approach for integration of individual skills from the organizational level begins at the design process wherein the organizational leader or manager selects growth initiatives. The organizational leader or manager in the arranging process brings together all the resources necessary for that initiative. Additionally, the organizational manager or leader motivates the mentors, coaches, and the individuals themselves influencing commitment to the development process. Last, the organizational manager or leader assures accountability in the process. Distinguishing senior NCOs experiences applies to organizations looking to develop skills and understand influences in situations of development, or initiatives for leader growth. Leading and managing is a social practice. Making sense of the environment within which development occurs helps leaders and managers shape their own understanding and knowledge to enhance or build upon existing skills. A manager and leader's knowledge and experiences with strategies for development allow flexibility, adaptability, and agility when performing in challenging environments. Senior NCOs described their perceptions regarding development and influences in that environment and evaluation of growth strategies.

Development Environment

Senior NCO's descriptions of the environment for development had many facets. Understanding that equipping leaders with the capacity to be flexible, adaptive, and agile in complex and uncertain environments depends upon aligning the leader development doctrine and a variety of strategies (see Figure 1). Senior NCOs described mentoring as the most impactful to learning development and building confidence in being flexible, adaptive, and agile (Hollis, 2017). Findings also confirmed that leaders' beliefs of coaching provided the motivation to enhance one's skills (Hollis, 2017). A coaching approach to developing skills has a stronger focus on self-awareness and accountability. Coaching puts the onus on leaders to take responsibility for identifying their own goals and objectives and working with the coach who offers guidance and sets critical challenges.

Interpretations of a study conducted with mid and senior-level managers also concluded coaching relationships, workshops, and a combination of strategies that provided feedback were valuable to enhancing greater levels of agility (Joiner & Josephs, 2007). Suggesting that strategies such as multisource feedback, mentoring, and coaching generate a consciousness of self-efficacy about learning and one's capacity. These strategies affected senior non-commissioned officers' self-awareness by providing opportunities for exposure to different perspectives on being flexible, adaptive, and agile in one's perceptions, assessment, and execution of a course of action. Civilian managers confirmed growth strategies developed personal commitment to conscious self-awareness (Joiner & Josephs, 2007). Senior NCOs expressed that mentoring and coaching were the most effective in facilitating the learning of skills. Senior leaders' experiences were indicative of the importance of the growth strategies for learning, understanding, and synthesizing experiences in both garrison and combat situations. Enhancing or growing leader skills ultimately requires connecting a myriad of developmental strategies in the U.S. Army's arsenal that provides valuation, stimulation, and encouragement to prepare senior NCOs to succeed in complex ever-changing situations. (see Figure 1).

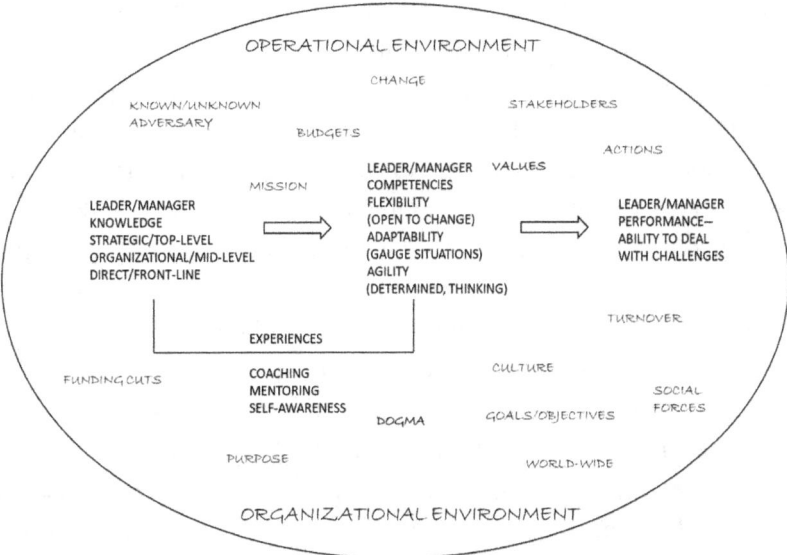

Figure 1. Knowledge and experiences, enhance and build competencies impacting performance. Adapted from *Flexible, adaptive, and agile leaders: A qualitative case study of experiences in leading and development*, by Hollis 2017, Retrieved from ProQuest Dissertations and Theses Global. (UMI No. 10615689)

Social, Culture, Context, and Dogma in Development Environment

Constructive development theory proposes that social relationships provide avenues for growth, interpretation of practices, and understanding. Senior NCOs ascribed this ability to their experiences and relationships with mentors and coaches and not necessarily to other initiatives deemed development (Hollis, 2017). Senior NCOs' experiences with some growth strategies produced mixed and confusing results that led to an unwillingness to invest time and effort (Hollis, 2017). Much of what senior leaders described was a result of their operational experiences and from strategies such as mentoring and coaching, which is important for understanding the influences of context in developing leaders (Hollis, 2017). The U.S. Army continued to establish a leader development framework during a time of multiple deployments and persistent conflict, leaders remained challenged to cultivate environments that reinforce and build commitment to activities, strategies, and instruments for development.

Senior NCOs obtained meaning and understanding through the organization's doctrine, values, attitudes, and purpose. Dogma such as the warrior ethos, soldier's creed, and NCO creed extended military culture and identity, and offered a level of understanding to leaders. A senior leaders' attitude is important. Skills of flexibility, adaptability, and agility are translatable, whether in a civilian environment or in the military. Findings in the case study indicated a lack of balance among growth strategies (i.e., operational, institutional, and self-development) to develop skills (Hollis, 2017). Additionally, at the organizational level, the findings indicated a lack of understanding of the development framework and various strategies or instruments for learning because of operational tempo (Hollis, 2017). Leaders at all levels must grasp the reasons for the strategy and have confidence that the strategy has merit and worth the undertaking. The refractive thinker challenges the complexity in development by moving from the described attitudes and beliefs to actions that achieve organizational goals and objectives. The refractive thinker® considers how variables of diversity, generation differences, managing and transferring knowledge, and technology are situated within the development environment.

Evaluation of Growth Strategies

The Hollis (2017) research sought senior NCO's evaluation of coaching and multi-source feedback and self-awareness. When considering their experiences with coaching as a strategy for growth and development, senior NCOs considered coaching a two-way street (Hollis, 2017). Both the coach and the coachee must have the same perception of intent and an awareness about what they are trying to accomplish to have a positive effect in the relationship. Additional thoughts of senior leaders included the amount of time it takes to coach an individual, as well as whether the individual is a follower, subordinate, or peer. Senior leaders still considered coaching important for enhancing ones' skills (Hollis, 2017).

Advantages of multisource feedback of all participants in the study offered that self-assessment was a continuous activity and validated their beliefs (Hollis, 2017). Senior NCO's reflections of feedback, mentoring, and coaching made them self-aware and increased their knowledge and skills personally and professionally. Several senior NCOs reflected on self-motivation as essential, that individuals must want to be a leader. Senior leaders' beliefs and awareness can lead to a change of behaviors or actions if the individual is internally motivated to enhance skills essential to being flexible and adaptive to challenging situations (Hollis, 2017). Therefore, relationships created through interactions with mentors and coaches and through formal and informal feedback are the most conducive to developing skills.

The importance for leader development must come from the most senior Army leaders down through each level of officer and noncommissioned officer. According to Schermerhorn (2014), strategic leaders underestimate the importance of their part in and the engagement necessary in the process of leader development. Strategic leaders must know and understand the leader development model and process. Strategic leaders must embody, display, and underwrite the proper conduct and reinforce the appropriate behaviors. Without this example represented from the highest levels of leadership to the lowest, organizations lose support for growth initiatives and development efforts (Longenecker & Insch, 2018).

The culture of the organization is an important factor to consider when enhancing skills of flexibility, adaptability, and agility. Both senior managers and leaders in civilian and military organizations attempt to cultivate a culture that includes tools such as coaching and mentoring and believed leaders should not just give lip service to understanding or knowing development processes. Leaders must use strategies and instruments to have trust in the process and trust in the feedback for leader awareness and growth or enhancement of skills.

Road Mapping Development

Organizational leader development programs vary and the extent that leaders grow and enhance skills depend upon knowledge and experiences with growth initiatives. Strategic leader's support of and for development to include their feelings, measures, and controls is important. Development strategies must account for attitudes, beliefs, dogma, and the context within which learning occurs to cultivate leader skills. The organizational culture and climate must also be supportive of both men and women (Hollis, 2017). Comparable findings were found in a study of managers that within programs without support in their culture or the climate that did not value or have the trust in development processes, results were not positive. Organizational cultures that did not support strategies and instrument of learning were ineffective (Fulmer & Hanson, 2010). A shift in paradigms is imperative to an effective developmental process wherein leaders and managers rely on learning and growth from experiences through education and self-development sources.

A structured practice of development is necessary to reach levels of strategic competency inherent to all leaders. The process for learning and applying knowledge includes recognizing that knowledge cannot be a completely and clearly formulated undertaking.

TRADOC implemented procedures and models to develop leaders ready to engage demands throughout the span of military operations. The leader requirements model emphasizes learning and growth from a combination of operational, educational, and self-development experiences (Headquarters, Department of the Army, 2014). These measures curtail leaders' reliance on operational experiences as a main strategy for development. Additionally, Select, Train, Education, and Promote (STEP) represents a course of action of investment into senior NCOs providing institutional education as a progressive process for development (Headquarters, Department of the Army, 2014). Structured self-development, development plans, and other strategies are another component by which senior NCOs incorporate ongoing learning and growth (Headquarters, Department of the Army, 2014).

Development must extend throughout the organization and create environments wherein everyone knows what to do through initiatives that have assessment and support such as mentoring and coaching. These growth activities or strategies allow one to acquire self- awareness and confidence and a broader perspective of the organization. According to Milner, McCarthy and Milner, (2018) in a study of manager preferences 14.9% believed having access to examples of coaching in the organization increased employee performance. The refractive thinker suggests change at the organizational level where systems and process ensure development is a priority and appropriately resourced. Creating change in basic assumptions of leader and manager development, accounts for diversity, technology transference, knowledge management, and generational differences. Targeting the needs of the manager and leader is needed to understand the variables within the operational and organizational environment to design initiatives that provide feedback and support. Much like the refractive thinker, managers and leaders must be self-aware and harness the change in thinking to build commitment.

Final Comments

Leaders and manager must understand the elements within the organization that enhance and or distract from development as well as the initiatives that garner success. The similarities that exist between civilian and military organizations are many, whether it is the operational or the organizational environment, the levels of leading and or the levels of functioning. Managers and leaders need skills of flexibility, adaptability, and agility to improve affairs within the organization while providing engaged leadership. Military organizations like civilian organizations associate specific responsibilities to strategic, organizational and direct level leaders and to top-level, mid-level and front-line managers. Senior NCOs' role and level of responsibility corresponds to the role and level of responsibility of managers. The research established mentoring to be the most impactful to development and building confidence. Additionally, ascertaining the importance and role of strategic leaders and managers in the development process. Understanding that equipping leaders with the capacity to be flexible, adaptive, and agile in complex and uncertain environments depends upon aligning the leader development doctrine and the initiatives. Learning requires reflecting on one's experiences and received feedback. Mentoring, coaching, trust, feedback and increased self-awareness enhanced capability of senior NCOs to be flexible, adaptive, and agile in difficult and demanding situations. The development of manager and leader's skills of flexibility, adaptability, and agility is an ongoing exploration that affects a much wider audience. Cultivating a skill set affects all disciplines and industries, for profits, and nonprofits and the people who make decisions.

THOUGHTS FROM THE ACADEMIC ENTREPRENEUR

The problem to be solved:

- Distinguishing variables in the environment of development
- Evaluating strategies that develop skills in operational managers and leaders

The goals:

- Recognizing variables such as organizational culture, climate, dogma, and or traditions enhance or detract within the environment of development and application of strategies such as mentoring, coaching, and self-awareness to build a set of skills

The questions to ask:

- What makes the environment for development challenging?
- How can the organization set the conditions and leverage variables in the development environment?
- What strategies or techniques succeed in developing manager and leader skill sets?

Today's Business Application:

- Recognizing variables such as organizational culture, climate, dogma, and or traditions enhance or detract within the environment of development.
- Application of strategies such as mentoring, coaching, and self-awareness to build a set of skills.

REFERENCES

Bateman, T. S., Snell, S. A., & Konopaske, R. (2017). *Management: Leading and collaborating in the competitive world* (13th ed.). New York, NY: McGraw Hill.

Deloitte Consulting LLP and Bersin by Deloitte. (2014). *Global Human Capital Trends 2014*. [online]. Available at https://www2.deloitte.com/insights/us/en/focus/human-capital-trends/2014/hc-trends-2014-introduction.html

Fulmer, R. M., & Hanson, B. (2010). Developing leaders in high-tech firms-what's different and what works? *People and Strategy, 33*(3), 22-27. Retrieved from https://www.hrps.org/resources/people-strategy-journal/fall-2010/Pages/default.aspx

Headquarters, Department of the Army. (2000). *The Army training and leader development panel officer study report to the Army*. Washington, DC: Government Accounting Office. Retrieved from http://www.au.af.mil/au/awc/awcgate/army/atld-panel/off_report.pdf

Headquarters, Department of the Army. (2002). *The Army training and leader development panel NCO study report to the Army*. Washington, DC: Government Accounting Office. Retrieved from http://www.dtic.mil/docs/citations/ADA401192

Hollis, E. (2017). *Flexible, adaptive, and agile leaders: A qualitative case study of experiences in leading and development* (Doctoral dissertation). Retrieved from ProQuest Dissertations and Theses Global. (UMI No. 10615689)

Joiner, B., & Josephs, S. (2007). Developing agile leaders. *Industrial and Commercial Training, 39*(1), 35-42. http://dx.doi.org/10.1108/00197850710721381

Kahnweiler, W. M. (2013). Nonprofit leaders and organization development consultants: Caveat emptor. *Organization Development Journal, 31*(2), 54-61. Retrieved from https://isodc.org/OD_journal

Longenecker, C., & Insch, G. S. (2018) Senior leaders' strategic role in leadership development. *Strategic HR Review, 17*(3), 143-149. http://dx.doi.org/10.1108/SHR-02-2018-0014

Milner, J., McCarthy, G., & Milner, T. (2018) Training for the coaching leader: How organizations can support managers, *Journal of Management Development, 37*(2), 188-200. http://dx.doi.org/10.1108/JMD-04-2017-0135

Schermerhorn, J. R. (2014). *Exploring management*. San Francisco, CA: Wiley.

Thach, E., & Thompson, K. J. (2007) Trading places: Examining leadership competencies between for profit vs. public and non-profit leaders, *Leadership and Organization Development Journal, 28*, 356-375. http://dx.doi.org/10.1108/01437730710752229

Vane, M. A. (2011). New norms for the 21st century soldier. *Military Review, 91*(4), 16-24. Retrieved from http://usacac.army.mil/CAC2/MilitaryReview/

About the Author ...

Dr. Evelyn Hollis resides in the historic town of El Paso. Dr. Hollis retired after 28 years of service from the United States Army as a senior enlisted leader and advisor. Dr. Evelyn has a Doctor of Management (DM) in Organizational Leadership. Her undergraduate degrees include a Master of Arts (MA) in Human Resource Development and Management and a Bachelor of Science (BS) in Management. Dr. Evelyn is an assistant professor with the United States Army Sergeants Major Academy. Dr. Evelyn is also adjunct faculty at Park University and University of Phoenix. Dr. Evelyn's experience spans over 20 years in managing and leading organizations. Her research interests include leader and leadership development. Awards include U. S. Army Women's Foundation Hall of Fame Inductee for 2018.

To reach Dr. Evelyn Hollis for information or guest speaking, please contact her by **email: evelynhollis05@gmail.com**

CHAPTER 8

Methods to Reducing the Rate of Recidivism Among Women

Dr. Toscha L. Dickerson

The United States has the highest incarceration rate in the world with more than 2 million jail and prison inmates reported, more than any other country, according to Bureau of Justice Statistics (BJS, 2018). Mass incarceration began in the 1970s as the *War on Drugs* and increased through the years, surpassing the number of people incarcerated from the 1980s through the 1990s and currently in 2018 with over 2 million. Within the United States, there is an alarming gender disparity since the 1970's incarceration trends. According to BJS (2018), there is a reduction in the incarceration rate since 2016, however; almost all the decrease has been among men. Research indicated women becoming one of the fastest growing incarcerated population on a state and local level. By taking a closer look at specific data, one can determine which states lead the disparities. Once these women release, the question to ask is what happens when they reenter back into their communities; and what are the plans for them to succeed. How do we ensure they do not recidivate and cycle back into the criminal justice system? The goal of the Dickerson (2018) study was to look beyond correctional programs and explore the methods within the programs of nonprofit organizations assisting women in their struggles with the criminal justice system. Because of the growing rate of incarcerated women, leaders in nonprofit organizations and mutual help groups with a mission to support women, could benefit from utilizing methods effectively reducing the rate of recidivism. The purpose of this chapter is to discuss the effectiveness of methods of nonprofit organizations and alternative to incarceration programs and the benefits women receive compared to the programs within the correctional system. Using practices of refractive thinking will help to increase awareness of women's issues and understand the importance of community involvement.

Background Information

When there is a repeat cycle into incarceration and reentering into criminal activity, it is referred to as *recidivism*. Recidivism is the "re-arrest, re-conviction, and re-incarceration of an ex-offender" (Andrews, 2016, p. 5). Research determines the recidivism rate stands between 66-76% and have been for decades which means at some point those 66-76 people will find themselves rearrested or back in prison (Andrews, 2016). Therefore, determining the lack of resources and diversion programs for women while incarcerated could possibly lead to a reduce rate of women recidivating. Aside from mass incarceration, women's imprisonment requires more attention because of the blatant ways in which prisons and jails failed women and their families (Sawyer, 2018). Incarcerated women face different issues than men; prison can inflate those issues and make them worse (Sawyer, 2018).

According to Sawyer (2018), there are 35 states listing women's prison population growing, while there is a reduction in the men's population. The growth of female imprisonment outnumbered men by 2 to 1 between 1980 and 2014; 1.2 million women were under supervision within the criminal justice system, according to Carson (2015). Statistics indicated that between 2000 and 2014, the rate of imprisonment in state and federal prisons declined for African American women, while the rate among white women increased (Carson, 2015). According to Covington (2000), the increased incarceration of women seems to be the result of different dynamics that shaped the U.S. criminal policies over decades to include: government policies, harsh sentencing as a response to internal issues, and state and federal mandates.

Many African American women in the criminal justice system are poor, uneducated, and unskilled (Carson, 2015). They come from impoverished neighborhoods, raised by single parents or in foster homes. Women are more susceptible than men to commit crimes to obtain money to purchase drugs. Therefore, exploring effective strategies to reduce prison population can help women in their journey not to return to prison.

Disparities of Women and Men Inmates

BJS (2018), indicates that women are arrested primarily for drug or property offenses and not violent crimes. Reviewing data from previous research concluded economical differences exist of incarcerated women earning less wages than men in prison and that women institutions do not meet the educational or vocational request for programs. A study conducted by Covington (2000), indicated inequalities existing between male and female drug offenders that affects their incarceration, treatment and reentry. Covington also indicated the criminal justice system had 6,300 women incarcerated in federal prison for drug related crimes. The question to ask is how women receive treatment for specific crimes. Research indicated mutual help groups and clinical services addressing women issues are more effective for women than traditional programs. Thus per, Covington,

> A major advantage of mutual-help groups for women is that they are free and, in most urban communities, readily available throughout most parts of the day. It is in this respect that they are most unlike conventional problem-solving techniques, whereby help is provided only on occasion, almost exclusively as a response to a specific request from an individual. These

programs can also create a safe environment, which is an essential element for recovery from trauma. (p. 2)

Organizations that provides mutual help base programs allow women to grow and be supportive of each other while creating a caring community.

The first step in helping women to reform and succeed acknowledges first and foremost that a gender difference exists that requires appropriate services and treatment focused on women. It is not a one size fits all type of service. Researchers indicated further disparities found between male and female inmates in terms of women imprisoned in maximum security facilities that have all levels of criminal offenses combined without any considerations and men assigned to prisons based on current offense, previous offense history, and psychological profiles. According to Braithwaite, Treadwell, and Arriola (2005), women inmates with disciplinary actions of the same infraction of their male counterparts go unnoticed by male institutions and while women crimes are less violent, they seem to get higher disciplinary citations for frivolous infractions. Laws for criminal offenses apply equally to men and women during sentencing, however; the characteristics for women and their roles and responsibilities in the criminal activity are different (Covington, 2003).

There seems to be an emphasis on the punishment rather than the need to seek treatment for women to rebuild. Research indicated that a difference between the educational and vocational programs exist in which there are more state and federal programs for male inmates than there are for women at these institutions (Covington, 2003). The programs offered do not address the traumatic experiences women have faced that led them into the criminal justice system. There is a continuous need to expand more programs for women to provide them with a marketable skillset they can use when returning to their communities (Braithwaite et al., 2005). Other disparities noted are health care concerns, such as regular gynecological and breast examinations (Braithwaite et al., 2005). Prior to incarceration, many of the women lack health care, according to researchers, putting them at a higher risk of life-threatening illnesses such as HIV / AIDS and Hepatitis C (Braithwaite et al., 2005). Health matters that go untreated while incarcerated will remain after the inmate release; public health professionals suggests treatment is beneficial for the community for the incarcerated population to be properly examined before release (Braithwaite et al., 2005). Public health agencies, nonprofits, and correctional facilities collaborate to provide resources to support different types of health issues. Per research by View Associates (2006),

> Comprehensive, integrated, gender-specific care is essential for the many inmates who suffer from both mental health and substance abuse problems. Female inmates frequently have histories of physical and / or sexual abuse. Placement in mental health and/or substance abuse treatment programs–instead of incarceration–may be the most effective way to address health related problems and to reduce expensive incarceration costs. Community involvement through effective networks of nonprofit, community-based service providers capable of customizing programs and services to the needs and circumstances of target populations. (p. 15)

The collaboration of networks enables organizations involved to participate in the betterment of women's health.

Impact on Families With an Incarcerated Parent

According to the National Resource Center on Children and Families of the Incarcerated (2014), there are approximately 2.7 million children with an incarcerated parent. The effect of an incarcerated parent can be life changing for a child. When women are incarcerated, the imprisonment affects not only themselves, but their families as well. The impact of having an incarcerated mother can be harmful to a child. Sawyer (2018) provided findings to indicate that over half of women incarcerated have minor children and because of the time away from their mother, family ties are permanently disengaged. The emotional and behavioral impact on children having an incarcerated parent results to stress, fear, and sadness, according to La Vigne, Davies, and Brazzell (2008).

Forever Family is a national nonprofit organization that provides services to children whose parents are incarcerated. The organization offers transportation services to children, making it accessible for them to see their parents while incarcerated (Forever Family, 2017). Forever Family is successful in their programs because of the robust cognitive behavioral model implemented, proven to reduce the impact of parental incarceration on children (Forever Family, 2017). There is very little research to indicate children of incarcerated parents will follow the same criminal path. However, BJS (2018) reported that parental incarceration has an adverse reaction in children and children are three times the odds at becoming antisocial or a delinquent. Research conducted suggested children are subject to stigmatization when one of their parents is incarcerated and the child may be afraid that others will judge or tease them. The age of the child when the mother is in incarceration determines the level of severity for the traumatic experience. A study conducted to assess the impact of separation from parents indicated that half of the population of children tested identified as having trauma related stress (Kampfner, 1995). Forever Family is an organization standing in the gap to provide resources to help with issues children experience when a parent faces incarceration.

Section 115 of the 1996 Welfare Reform Act, *Temporary Assistance for Needy Families* (TANF), stipulates that persons convicted of a state or federal felony offense involving the use or sale of drugs are subject to a lifetime ban on receiving cash assistance and food stamps (Mauer, 2015). This ban does not represent felonies for violent crimes such as robbery or burglary. There is an option for states to modify this or opt out of the provision. As of 2015, there are three states that continues to enforce the lifetime ban and other states have amended to allow conditions. This was a punitive measure to end the *War on Drugs* of the 1990s; however, mass incarceration continues to impact low-income communities and the efforts to reduce recidivism (Paresky, 2017). Research indicated almost half of the incarcerated population has drug felony convictions on a state and federal level. If families are unable to apply for cash assistance or food stamps after release, the question is asked how they can care for their families while seeking employment. According to Paresky (2017), over half of previous incarcerated individuals reported they were unable to employ 1 year after their release.

The Adoption and Safe Families Act of 1997 (ASFA) is a federal legislation which consents to the termination of parental rights during a parent's sentencing, even if the parent can care for their child after release (Smyth, 2012). Because of support from child advocates and other organizations, states passed amendments to ASFA to provide leniency and to protect the parental rights of incarcerated parents. However, amending ASFA from a federal standpoint continues to keep families together after release, rather than depending on each state. Research demonstrated that removing children from their home and ASFA terminating parental rights from incarcerated parents can have negative effects on families. Consequently, alternative ways other than incarceration remains important for mothers. One approach is to search for organizations that offer programs that will satisfy court mandates while keeping mothers and their children together.

Mothers And Their Children (MATCH) is a nonprofit organization providing services to children with incarcerated mothers.

MATCH provides a home away from home visitation center where children can visit their mothers (MATCH, 2018). The organization provides parenting education, financial assistance for families, and psychological cognitive development for families. This organization supports the reunification of families as opposed to the AFSA mandate which terminates the parental rights of incarcerated parents.

Alternative Programs Used to Support Women

Housing Plus is a non-profit organization that provide tools women need to rebuild. Housing Plus has many programs offered to women; one of their successful programs is the *Drew House Program*. A case study conducted at the Drew House in New York implemented an Alternative To Incarceration (ATI) program. The Drew House is a permanent support program that allows women to live in a private apartment with their children who are homeless, have custody of their dependent children, suffers from substance abuse or mental illness and have been charged with a felony (Smyth, 2012). With onsite supervision and fulfilling court mandates, the program includes therapeutic treatment that women can successfully complete within 18 months resulting in the dismissal of felony charges and alleviating the separation of families (Smyth, 2012). Columbia University researchers did an audit of the Drew House and their findings determined the program to be effective in which other organizations should model (Smyth, 2012). The strategies implemented within the Drew House program is successful and exemplifies the importance of support and family.

The Urban Institute (2008) conducted a study of women returning home from prison and concluded a high percentage needed assistance with housing, financial, and employment support services compared to men, and that women also have specific needs related to trauma, substance use, physical health, and parental stress. Based upon an environmental model, wraparound services are the use of strengths and resources received from professionals, family, friends, and community members committed to work collaboratively to address severe emotional and behavioral needs of women and children (Sawyer, 2018). Nonprofit organizations that implement wraparound services show results in reduced cost of hospital, residential treatment care, reduction in emotional and behavioral problems, and increased community alignment, according to Texas System of Care (2018).

The Center for Alternative Sentencing and Employment Services (CASES) is another nonprofit organization that provides alternatives to incarceration programs in the City of New York since the 1960s. They provide services that are cost-effective for ATI and Alternative to Detention (ATD) for both youth and women who suffer from trauma and mental illnesses (Cases, 2018). An evidence-based approach to include responsive approaches unique to the risks and needs related to possible recidivism, the program targets the following:

- Risk and needs assessment, Individual and group counseling,
- Family services,
- Substance abuse monitoring and counseling,
- Cognitive behavioral therapy,
- Housing Services,
- Education and Employment services, and
- Mental health treatment. (Cases, 2018, p. 1)

The success of the program includes nearly 4,000 participants of youth and women given an alternative. The program serves to improve lives while reducing the costs of government funds spent on correctional costs, public safety as well as reducing recidivism

(Cases, 2018). NewStart is a short-term alternative to incarceration program that assists of those with misdemeanor charges recommended to serve a minimum number of days in jail (Cases, 2018). The nonprofit organization CASES created the program to conduct individual and group cognitive behavioral interventions (Cases, 2018). Because of the short sentencing and costs that occur with processing and transporting an inmate, it is cost effective to have these offenders report to an ATI. As of 2018, the NewStart program has relieved over 1700 men and women from short-term jail sentences (Cases, 2018). There are other ATI programs that assist in reducing recidivism rates and addressing specific needs of individuals; however, the need is greater than the options available. The nonprofit organizations' methods listed above provides evidence-based criteria to be an effective way to promote and support healthier individuals, families, and the reduction of costs associated with incarceration.

Conclusion

This chapter provided a summary of what prison reform entails and a glimpse into the criminal justice correctional system. The truth is, no one can force rehabilitation and transformation; an individual must be willing to see the change for themselves. There are disparities that exist throughout the criminal justice system and finding an alternative to incarceration program can be an effective way to mitigate risks, costs, and inequalities. Nonprofit organizations with gendered based programs and mutual help groups are important in understanding and recognizing the dynamics of a gendered society. Women face some of life's greatest challenges specifically because of their gender such as domestic violence, sexual abuse, and sexual assault, in addition to having the responsibility of being the custodial parent (Bloom et al., 2004). Research indicated that the path to crime for women is because of the need to survive abuse and poverty. Therefore, there is a need for the criminal justice system to acknowledge the differences between male and female inmates to sentence appropriately based on socially, behaviorally, and cultural differences.

Women who commit a crime should not experience penalties for the rest of their lives after completing their court orders. Denying someone access to food and housing benefits because of a drug felony conviction is barbaric and forces them to find other ways to provide for their families. By using cognitive techniques and gendered base programs, refractive thinkers may be able to enhance their problem-solving skills. Research supports cognitive behavioral programs that are gendered base, providing the necessary treatment and support for women and children to become successful. The Lahr (2018) study presents an overview of a few programs that focuses on social entrepreneurship and are successful in the path of reentry and can be used as a model for other organizations. The reunification of families should be the goal for communities and nonprofit organizations to implement methods that assist in the growth and safety of ex-offenders re-entering into their neighborhoods. Research throughout this chapter identified nonprofit organizations that focus on women and understanding their needs to rehabilitate and not re-incarcerate.

THOUGHTS FROM THE ACADEMIC ENTREPRENEUR

The problem to be solved:

- How to reduce the rate of recidivism among women
- Recognizing and dismantling the inequalities that exist between women and male inmates

The goals:

- Develop an understanding that the needs of women differ from men both physically and psychologically
- Implement gender-based programs to recognize and assist women who suffer with mental illness and abuse prior to entering the criminal justice system
- Provide and teach skills women can use to be successful in seeking employment after release

The questions to ask:

- How do we implement more alternative to incarceration programs?
- What price will society pay when we incarcerate rather than rehabilitate?
- What changes can the government make to assist in prison reform?
- How can the criminal justice system alleviate sentencing for drug related crimes?

Today's Business Application:

- Leaders who understand the need for gender-based activities and programs without being discriminatory, despite socioeconomic disparities, can effectively support and respond to individuals in a holistic manner.

- Create an environment that is free of prejudices, safe, and respectful.
- Implement policies and programs that promote healthy relationships between families and communities.

REFERENCES

Andrews, E. (2016). Making the most of your time: Beating the odds of recidivism. Cambridge, OH: Christian Publishing House.

Biddy, E. (2004). Women behind bars: Hard time, getting harder. Retrieved from http://www.diversityatwork.com/news/feb00/news_usa3.html.

Braithwaite, R., Treadwell, H., & Arriola, K. (2005). Health disparities and incarcerated women: A population ignored. American Journal of Public Health, 95, 1679-1681. doi:10.2105/AJPH.2005.065375

Bloom, B., Owen, B., & Covington, S. (2004). Women offenders and the gendered effects of public policy. Review of Policy Research, 21(1), 31-48. doi:10.1111/j.1541-1338.2004.00056.x

Bureau of Justice Statistics (BJS). (2018). 2018. U.S. Department of Justice. Retrieved from https://www.bjs.gov

Carson, E. (2016). Prisoners in 2015. U.S. Department of Justice. Retrieved from https://www.bjs.gov/content/pub/pdf/p15.pdf.

Cases organization. (2018). Retrieved from https://www.cases.org/

Covington, S. S. (2000). Helping women recover: A comprehensive integrated treatment model. Alcohol Treatment Quarterly, 18(3), 99-111.

Covington, S. S. (2003). A woman's journey home: Challenges for female offenders. The Urban Institute, 1-32. Retrieved from https://www.stephaniecovington.com/assets/files/3.pdf

Forever Family Organization. (2018). For our families. Retrieved from http://www.foreverfam.org

Kampfner, C. J. (1995). Post-traumatic stress reactions in children of imprisoned mothers: Children of incarcerated parents. New York, NY: The Russell Sage Foundation.

Lahr, D. C. (2018). Piercing the cycle of recidivism: A self-study to inform social entrepreneurship education as a path to successful reentry for previously incarcerated African American women (Doctoral dissertation). Retrieved from ProQuest Dissertations & Theses Global. (Accession No. 10785498)

La Vigne, N., Davies, E., & Brazell, D. (2008). Broken bonds: Understanding and addressing the needs of children with incarcerated parents. The Urban Institute. Retrieved from https://www.urban.org/sites/default/files/publication/31486/411616-Broken-Bonds-Understanding-and-Addressing-the-Needs-of-Children-with-Incarcerated-Parents.PDF

MATCH Organization. (2018). Strengthening the families of incarcerated moms. Retrieved from http://www.mothersandtheirchildren.org/about_us.aspx

Messina, N., Burdon, W., Hagopian, G., & Prendergast, M. (2001). Predictors of prison-based treatment outcomes: A comparison of men and women participants. American Journal of Drug and Alcohol Abuse, 32(1), 7–28. doi:10.1080/00952990500328463

Maurer, M., & McCalmont, V. (2015). A lifetime of punishment: The impact of the felony drug ban on welfare benefits. The Sentencing Project. Retrieved from https://www.sentencingproject.org

National Resource Center on Children & Families of the Incarcerated. (2014). Incarcerated parents. Retrieved from https://nrccfi.camden.rutgers.edu/

Paresky. M. (2017). Changing welfare as we know it, again: Reforming the welfare reform act to provide

all drug felons' access to food stamps. Boston College Law Review, 58, 1659. Retrieved from https://lawdigitalcommons.bc.edu/bclr/vol58/iss5/6

Sawyer, W. (2018). The gender divide: Tracking women's state prison growth. Policy Initiative. Retrieved from http://www.prisonpolicy.org

Smyth, J. (2012). Dual punishment: Incarcerated mothers and their children. Columbia Social Work Review. 3, 32-45. Retrieved from https://cswr.columbia.edu/article/dual-punishment-incarcerated-mothers-and-their-children

Texas System of Care. (2018). Wraparound services. Retrieved from http://www.txsystemofcare.org/wraparound/

Urban Institute. (2008). Health and prisoner reentry: How physical, mental, and substance abuse conditions shape the process of reintegration. Justice Policy Center. Retrieved from https://www.urban.org/sites/default/files/publication/31491/411617-Health-and-Prisoner-Reentry.PDF

View Associates. (2006). Philanthropic opportunities in correctional health care. Retrieved from https://www.langeloth.org

About the Author...

Dr. Toscha L. Dickerson resides in the historic town of Houston, Texas. Dr. Toscha is a university professor on faculty with Liberty University and American InterContinental University (AIU). Dr. Dickerson teaches Business and Supply Chain Management courses to graduate students. She is also a certified professional life coach, offering expertise as a professional coach to her students. She is the founder of S.T.R.E.S.S.O.U.T. A women's organization that provides support services to previously incarcerated women. Dr. Dickerson is also a founding board member of Rève Preparatory Charter School for children in grades K–8.

Dr. Toscha is an active member of Delta Mu Delta Honor Society. She is also an author known for her book titled Sisterhood Traveling the Scarlet Road to an Authentic Life. Additional published works include her dissertation: *An analysis of disruptions in aerospace/defense organizations affecting the supply chain.*

To reach Dr. Toscha L. Dickerson for information on this study, reducing recidivism among women, or guest speaking, please visit her **websites: http://www.drtoschadickerson.com http://www.women4us.org** or **e-mail: toschad1@gmail.com**

CHAPTER 9

Nonprofit: U.S. Leaders' Experiences with Developing Global Networks

Dr. Samuel Hayes, Jr.

Leaders can understand life (e.g., religious) through social networks (Everton, 2015). Everton (2015) noted through relationships (a) leaders recruit followers, (b) followers spread ideas, and (c) leaders tear down other networks. These networks are powerful, and their leaders are influential. Obama and Graham, for instance, who developed global networks, exemplified the relational leadership style in complex environments through non-specified paths (Cogburn & Espinoza-Vasquez, 2011; Lindsay, 2006). Nonprofit leaders need to address global network development in a dynamic world to advance organizational goals and provide an opportunity for scholars (Dinh et al., 2014) and practitioners (Cullen & Yammarino, 2014) to improve global network development. This research focused on relationships that strengthen global networks (Hayes, 2018). The findings yielded some new insights that provided leaders with a spectrum of actions to build global networks internally. In this chapter of The Refractive Thinker®, I present an overview of the Hayes (2018) study of global network development, contributing to the scholarly dialogue to assist nonprofit leaders with their goals.

Nonprofits leaders' success often depends on their ability to manage relationships (Dutton & Ragins, 2017). These relationships are essential to social networks and relational leadership. Leaders take time to build and maintain a variety of relationships with principal stakeholders, resulting in positive impacts, such as increased trust, devoted commitment, and stronger cooperation (Abosagf, Yen, & Barnes, 2016). For example, face-to-face interactions between leaders often allow individuals to confirm common ground, that leads to increased interaction and creates the path to increased involvement (Fairhurst & Conaughton, 2014). This type of relational investment leads to a competitive advantage with trust (Fang, Palmatier, Scheer, & Li, 2008), and communication (Moorman, Zaltman, & Deshpande, 1992). The advantage aids leaders with creating a vision (Sarros, Cooper, & Santora, 2011), and raising funds (Mollick, 2014). As a result, nonprofit leaders can improve their communities through relationships.

Failure to address these relationships leads to adverse outcomes, such as organization closures from the inability to maintain close personal relationships with customers (Wang, Gopal, Shankar, & Pancras, 2015), a failure to achieve goals (Nyaga, Lynch, Marshall, & Ambrose, 2013), and receiving a negative stigma for not being successful (Singh, Corner, & Pavlovich, 2015). Additionally, these nonprofit leaders' mishandled relationships can lead to disenfranchised followers and a chaotic community (Austin & Pinkleton, 2015). This decline demonstrated a link between leaders' actions and their followers. In other words, these relational leaders' leadership styles are tested regarding vision attainment, and resource acquisition, directly related to relational management. These relational leaders' span of influence is extensive and life changing for their followers and communities.

The problem is a lack of understanding of how nonprofit leaders' actions influence relationships in their social networks (e.g., environment), which can be either better or worse for their members and communities. Within the United States, the problem is that leaders use various leadership styles to develop social networks that yield poor results (Christerson & Flory, 2017). Leveraging individual leader traits in implementing transformational actions, leaders do not have a prescribed way to build networks.

These leaders lack practical ways to sustain these networks over time and across international boundaries while remaining a closely tied resilient network. Therefore, these nonprofit leaders are critical to study with the need to add them to the literature regarding global network dynamics and leadership challenges (Carpenter, Li, & Jiang, 2012; Fransen et al., 2015). The goal of this chapter is to explore U.S. leaders' experiences in their development of global social networks in specific areas across two or more countries in 2017, therefore understanding the broader phenomenon of global leadership dynamics.

Conceptual Framework

In Figure 1 below, the conceptual domain framework represents the fundamental concepts. This figure shows the interconnected domains studied among relational leadership theory (RLT), social network analysis (SNA), and global social networks. Hayes (2018) filled the literature gap with this study, contributing to the broader knowledge of the interplay among these scholarly fields (Balkundi & Kilduff, 2006; Carpenter et al., 2012; Everton, 2015).

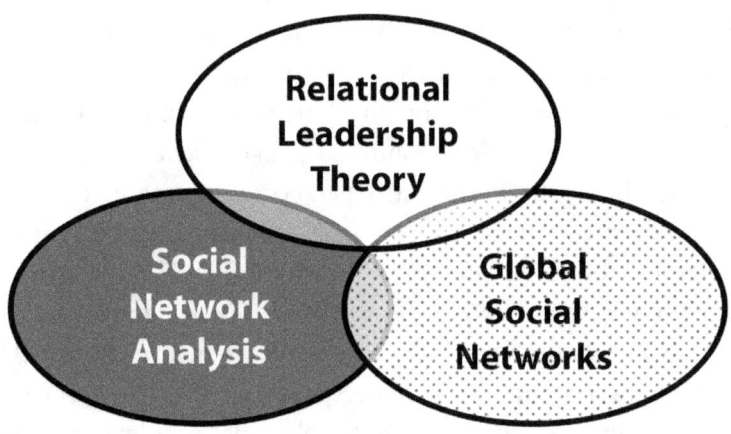

Figure 1. Conceptual domain framework.

Exploring the space in between leader and follower, Hayes (2018) attempted to unlock how U.S. leaders used relational leadership theory in practice. RLT provided the theoretical foundations for the social process by which leadership organizes, influences, and evolves the social order (Uhl-Bien, 2006). SNA provided the tools to illuminate these relationships to select which leaders were the most socially connected (Everton, 2015). The exploratory qualitative inquiry was the method used to explore the leaders' experiences to gain insights into current practices with developing global social networks and assisted with answering the research question: *What are U.S. leaders' experiences with relational leadership in developing global social networks?*

LITERATURE REVIEW

Relational Leadership Theory

RLT presented the opportunity to investigate the relational dynamics of leadership (Uhl-Bien, 2006), as a seminal work. RLT explored relational dynamics by focusing on the social practices that encompass leadership and the organization. RLT aided with social influence that contributes to social order and change that encompasses dual perspectives (a) entity (e.g., individual) focused on personal relationships and their attributes and (b) relational (e.g., collective) viewed leadership as social construction (Uhl-Bien, 2006). Uhl-Bien (2006), the entity perspective, explored exchanges between the two-way influences from relationships dealing with leaders and followers (Graen & Scandura, 1987); whereas, the relational view included exploration of the collective dynamic (e.g., social network) to construct social order and change (Uhl-Bien, 2006). Incorporating both perspectives within the framework made RLT unique and attractive to relational scholars and as the starting point for the Hayes (2018) study.

RLT's overarching framework derived from two elements (Uhl-Bien, 2006). The first element, Uhl-Bien (2006), the entity perspective, focused on individual viewpoints of cognition, attributes, behaviors, and being organized to reach goals and gain organizational influence (Uhl-Bien, 2005, 2006). Uhl-Bien (2006) assumed, from the entity perspective, that the relationship was the outcome that would answer the question of how people relate to each other and work together; specifically, through the individual bonds between another (e.g., a person, group, organization, and network). Additionally, determining if these bonds were strong or weak relationships or ties (Granovetter, 1973). Based on this assumption, the Hayes (2018) study included the exploration of this important question from the leaders' described experiences with relationships at the entity (e.g., individual) and relational (e.g., collective) levels.

Second, Uhl-Bien (2006) described the relational perspective as a collective level, which assumed social reality occurred within relationships (Hosking, 2007; Hosking & Bouwen, 2000) and emerged through new approaches, attitudes, and change (Uhl-Bien, 2006). This perspective viewed organizations as a social fabric or a network that interacts with the organization and the external environment (Uhl-Bien, 2006). Uhl-Bien assumed, from the relational perspective, that the structure was the regular interaction patterns of an organization and resided in the rules by which they organized. Following this assumption, the Hayes (2018) study also included the exploration of this question from the leaders' described experiences of evolving the social order of their organization.

When combining views, a common thread exists—relationships are a social process—only from different philosophical positions (e.g., modern and postmodern). Relational leadership is the focus of the overarching framework, as a process of social influence. RLT's constructs produce change and coordination (Uhl-Bien, 2006). This interactive process yields influence at both levels between partners, collaborators, and participants. Interestingly, if one would apply Uhl-Bien's (2006) RLT framework to history dating from biblical to modern times, could illuminate new insights.

Social Network Analysis

Since the 1990s, SNA's popularity increased in organizational management research. SNA has been utilized to understand turnover (Kilduff & Krackhardt, 1994), unethical behavior (Brass, Butterfield, & Skaggs, 1998), job performance (Sparrowe, Liden, Wayne, & Kraimer, 2001), creativity (Burt, 2004), innovation (Obstfeld, 2005), and promotion (Burt, 2009). SNA also aided with the study of leadership (a) SNA can model relationships patterns, (b) SNA can represent the distribution of leadership is distributed, and (c) SNA can identify the leadership emergence (Emery, Calvard, & Pierce, 2013). Network analyses became a standard diagnostic and prescriptive tool for organizations and could aid leaders in their developmental efforts. In the Hayes (2018) study, SNA provided a visualization of the relationships defined by RLT and illuminated these relationships from a network perspective (Everton, 2016), which was the next step in the conceptual framework.

SNA consisted of tools to help understand networks, comprised of relationships and structures (Dempwolf & Lyles, 2011). SNA principles include the assumption that individuals were social and connected to others through links (e.g., ties) regarding network theory (Wasserman & Faust, 1994). Analyst used SNA to visualize emerging social formations at the individual (i.e., micro), group (i.e., meso), and institutions (e.g., macro) levels. According to Everton (2012), the primary goal was to use metrics to understand the network better. Some other examples of SNA were Kerbs (2002) who examined the 9/11 hijacker network; and Krackhardt and Hanson (1993) who studied informal networks between influential managers. These examples highlighted the discovery power of SNA, illuminating hidden insights (e.g., dark network leaders and the social capital of managers) that were not apparent. Specifically, Hayes (2018) noted finding relational leaders might be a challenge if one was not familiar with apostolic networks defining attributes and SNA could illuminate them.

Apostolic Networks

Networked Christianity increased, since 2005; specifically, a global network called the New Apostolic Reformation (NAR) that was the fastest-growing network in the West and the global South (Christerson & Flory, 2017). Following Genesis 1:26 mandate, the NAR's overarching goal was for the church to have dominion over all governments and societies, in preparation for the establishment of God's Kingdom on earth. The central premise took a proactive approach to establishing dominion before to the rapture (e.g., Jesus Christ's return), rather than a reactive approach to establishing rule after the rapture (e.g., during Jesus Christ's millennial reign). Exploring this paradigm, the NAR and other Christian groups used networks to expand their influence. U.S. leaders were central to the conceptual framework and in exploring their experiences with developing networks.

For example, Johnson and Ross (2009) stated that the NAR has 369 million members, and O'Reggio (2012) claimed that network continued to grow at a rate of nine million per year. NAR was a loosely bound multinetwork, with no specified leader. This network derived from Charismatics and Pentecostals (O'Reggio, 2012), and continued to grow in the diminishing Protestant domain due to precipitous institutionalization. Creating a setting inviting to failing denominations, and providing a home for the disenfranchised self-governing churches, NAR built an international network. This network encompassed churches worldwide, businesses, educational institutions, and media outlets.

Terminology and concepts. The term *apostle* was more than a title, a brand, franchise, a benevolent dictator, or a club (Cook, 2012). This type of leader, an apostle, was an ambassador chosen by God for a specific mission in an unclaimed territory (Cook, 2012; Weaver, 2016). In other words, Jesus Christ's representative on the earth and function as generals and governors. Kelly (2016) posited, "God gives apostles divine strategies to lead in battle, to change direction, to establish righteousness and displace the works of the enemy" (para. 5). Apostles' functions have been used to illustrate ruling as a governor, in the Old Testament, (Neh. 2:5-6, King James Version) to establish and to maintain order. Nehemiah became the king's authorized representative-ambassador to rebuild Jerusalem (Cottle, 2015). Nehemiah, as governor, exercised the authority necessary to accomplish his Kingdom assignment (Cottle, 2015).

These apostles functioned in the church and operated in the marketplace. These marketplace apostles served as industry captains, CEOs, and leaders within their sphere influence (Marshall & Walker, 2011; Wagner, 2000). They bring resources—finances, skills, knowledge, and abilities—into the house of God, they led in their assigned territories. This leadership could take place within advancing policy on critical issues within the community or leveraging technology to further God's message in media, business, and education. Without their keen insight into specific spheres or protocols, just like Moses approaching Pharaoh to let God's people go or David learning from Jonathan on Kingdom etiquette, highlighting key opportunities.

Apostles lead apostolic networks. Anklam (2007) described networks as (a) *horizontal*, a network of peers or a fellowship; (b) *vertical*, a hierarchical or covering organization led by a single person; and (c) *functional*, a network focused on a function. In these networks, Kelly (2018a) posited that leaders build networks to have fellowship and to share insights, knowledge, wisdom, and strategies with peers. Additionally, Kelly (2018b) argued some principal leader characteristics: proven character, Christ-focused; priority, family first and ministry second; submission, equally to each member; accountability, based on transparent relationships; discipling people, build lives; and relationships, autonomous and self-governed. Apostles who are strategic and entrepreneurial that lead relational networks.

Data Analysis

The population for this research included the U.S. Region, a junior member of the Global Kingdom. U.S. leaders in the U.S. Region are nonprofit leaders (e.g., religious) and business leaders; they also deal with similar organizational issues as business leaders in corporate America (Cohall & Cooper, 2010). For example, both organizational structures have similar components to include: leaders (e.g., Chief Executive Officer (CEO) and Apostle / Bishop), followers (e.g., employees and members), who use resources (e.g., people and money) to accomplish goals. Apostolic leaders design strategies and focus on relationships (Kelly, 2016), which is essential to nonprofits and this research because of the central role relationships play in religion (Everton, 2015; Finke & Stark, 1988; Iannaccone, 1994; Iannaccone, Stark, & Finke, 1998).

Hayes (2018) explored 10 U.S. leaders' networks to understand the relationship between U.S. leaders' experiences and global network development. The Ekklesia network contained religion and family relationships; the Marketplace consisted of education, media, government, arts and entertainment, and relationships. For example, the sample group of 10 leaders' influence, at the individual level, expanded from the 10 U.S. leaders to over 500 people with over 1500 relationships because of the U.S. leaders' connections with other people. Hayes determined (a) in the Ekklesia individual network, U.S. leaders were central and expanded their relationships with other key leaders; (b) in the Marketplace individual network,

U.S. leaders were also central and expanded their relationships with organizational leaders; and (c) the combined individual network highlighted U.S. leaders being central of all clusters in the networks, indicating that the Ekklesia network was more prominent.

In addition, Hayes (2018) depicted the 10 U.S. leaders combined collective network. The vastness of combined individual network expanded from the 10 U.S. leaders to over 680 nodes with over 540 leaders and with over 140 organizations because of their connections with other people and organizations. Hayes concluded that in the Ekklesia collective network, organizations were central and on the edges of the network, there were a significant amount of organizations that had relationships clustered together, containing many leaders who wield much influence. The majority (e.g., approximately 85%) of the U.S. leaders were in the center of this collective network, which indicated that the organizations were more the focal point rather than the leaders.

Hayes (2018) noted several insights from the 10 U.S. leaders' demographics. The majority of this group was male, 90%, which represented the larger population and with 50% being older than 59 years. The leaders' valued higher education, indicated by eight of the 10 held doctoral degrees with several individuals having two doctoral degrees. Hayes determined 70% of these leaders operate from the Southern portion of the United States and projected their global influence outward from the closest to the farthest continent to the United States. However, under-explored continents were Asia, Australia, and Antarctica. These seasoned leaders had on average 30 years plus of leadership experience.

Additionally, Hayes (2018) gained insights from the 10 U.S. leaders' profile summaries with leadership styles and span of control. Some of the challenges facing the U.S. leaders are no prescribed methods, leadership styles, developmental steps, or prescribed paths. Interestingly, leaders self-described themselves as servant leaders, teachers, and developers; no leadership style was typical among the leaders, which suggests more unknown variables exist related to leadership. More important, U.S. leadership styles convey a lack of leadership prescription for network leaders.

Table 1 provides an overview of the research results. Depicted are the major themes that emerged from analysis of the data in response to each interview question. Based on the thematic analysis, Hayes (2018) synthesized five themes from 10 U.S. leaders' experiences with developing global networks. The first theme included a description of the context of networks, the second and third themes addressed RLT at the individual level, and the fourth and fifth themes covered the collective level of RLT.

TABLE 1. SUMMARY OF DATA ANALYSIS THEMES AND SUB-THEMES RESULTS

What are U.S. leaders' experiences with relational leadership in global social networks?

Level of Analysis	Data Analysis Theme	Sub-themes
Context	Networks	1. Ekklesia
		2. Marketplace
Individual	Key Network Relationships	1. Spiritual Family
		2. Emerging Leaders
Individual	Leadership Network Development	1. Build trust
		2. Educate, equip, and empower
		3. Leverage the network
Collective	Network Influence	1. Model the behavior
		2. Communication
Collective	Network Leadership Influence	1. Develop the family
		2. Foster trust
		3. Achieve the goal

Theme one, networks, leaders described characteristics of networks, Ekklesia and Marketplace, (e.g., size, scope, and effectiveness) and impacts of a global movement. For example, some of the U.S. leaders' goal was to (a) empower 4000 churches across the world, (b) leverage regional assets (e.g., Police, Medical, Immigration, and Church) to aid at-risk populations, and (c) influence a trans-denominational global apostolic network with 300 visionary U.S. leaders. Similarly, the leaders conveyed network effectiveness, deploying solutions from an Ekklesia prism into specific areas or leveraging Marketplace leaders' ability to measure results. These leaders' descriptions provided the frame to view all other themes.

Theme two, key network relationships, leaders described key traits of spiritual family members and organizational impacts of emerging leaders. For instance, leaders detailed the importance of family, fulfilling God's family mandate to multiply, as described in scripture (Gen 1:28), and transitioning servants into sonship with the goal reaching their density in God, which suggests submitting to a higher authority. The act of submission could allow for effective leadership because the leader's example was similar to the request of the follower. The leaders described emerging leaders' impact, creating powerful visions to drive the organization, and developing agile and adapt organizations responsive to changes in the environment. These leaders' descriptions provided insight into the first practical step at the individual level.

Theme three, leadership network development, leaders' knowledge covered investing in trust, managing accountability, and creating movements on a global scale to reach a common goal. Specifically, leaders built trust, as investing in trust strengthens a bond between the leader and the follower and holding followers accountable and motivated followers to reach higher goals. Leaders educated, equipped, and empowered others who resembled themselves. Additionally, leaders leveraged the network, mobilizing the network to create movements. These leaders' descriptions provided insight into the second practical step at the individual level.

Theme four, network influence, leaders indicated that shaping and enhancing the network occurs through written and verbal means from the individual to the collective network. Consider, as described by most of the leaders, modeling the behavior means following Jesus' example; they pattern their lives after the Bible, which inspires their followers in the network and communication, leaders conducted face-to-face conversions to advance video conferences to influence the network. These leaders' descriptions provided insights into the first practical step at the collective level.

Theme five, network leadership influence, leaders conveyed that developing a family identity, building a growth platform, and achieving kingdom goals. For example, most leaders detailed the importance of a sense of family, followers feel more like brothers and sisters versus co-labors, creating a family unit and a sense of belonging and leaders conveyed that fostering an environment of trust was the key for followers to grow and mature. Additionally, leaders described achieving the kingdom goal as Jesus' ultimate plan, because He never built an institution; Jesus always built a family. These leaders' descriptions provided insight into the final step at the collective level.

Conclusion

Hayes (2018) designed this study to answer the research question, *What are U.S. leaders' experiences with relational leadership in developing global social networks?* Not only did the study's findings answer the research question, but the results also addressed the need for the study. The significance of the study illustrated the relationship between theory (e.g., RLT, SNA, and GSN) and practice. Using the thematic data analysis process five themes emerged reflecting the developmental experiences of U.S. leaders, resulting in practical insights that U.S. leaders (a) invest in relationships and then leverage the network and (b) shape the network and achieve organizational goals. Followed by, new insights towards developing global networks: (a) identify / develop culture, (b) leverage culture, (c) create opportunities, and (d) exploit success, thereby addressing a gap in the literature.

Implications

The implications of this exploratory qualitative inquiry's findings could influence the development of new theories and add to the knowledge base in the field of organization and management. Nonprofit leaders, leadership and network scholars, and organizations and nonprofits may benefit from the findings of this study as well. Nonprofit leaders could apply the findings to enhance their understanding of their relational leaders and network development. These leaders embodied the entrepreneurial spirit and built these networks from nothing, which might illustrate how to develop networks from a nascent stage. Many ways exist that organizations might benefit from applying this information at the organizational level. For example, leaders could develop a global network focusing inwardly first on building leaders and then outwardly to thrive in the global environment to reach their organizational goals. Therefore, the implications of this research might help both organizations and leaders to develop successful relational networks.

The practical implications of this study are substantial considering that the problem involved finding ways to reach organizational goals, develop global networks, and expand organizational influence. The findings might provide substantial insights for leaders and organizations, specifically regarding leaders who (a) need relational skills to manage multiple networks, (b) identify key traits in followers to mentor into leaders, (c) need leadership skills to lead a network of networks, (d) evaluate the network to shape to the desired network, and (e) evaluate the sentiment of the network to align with network goals. Hayes (2018) posited the actions required for leaders and organizations to focus internally on developing robust, resilient networks.

There were some practical implications for the theme of the network. First, the 10 U.S. leaders' demographics provided a realistic picture that highlights a seasoned leader regarding age, education, and experience with global influence for nonprofit leaders. This type of leader acquired relational leadership experience, but the study does not indicate how to gain this experience. Second, the visualization of their experience through network diagrams at both levels provided network insights into the importance of centralization and a leader's ability to manage several networks which on average was four or fewer networks. To further this point, in the 10 U.S. leaders' profile summaries, no leader operated in all seven focus areas. However, the study did not indicate how these leaders maintained their multiple networks explicitly. Therefore, the networks theme highlighted that seasoned global leaders with the ability to manage several relational networks, take time to develop.

Recommendations for Future Research

Based on the responses of the U.S. leaders regarding their experiences with developing global networks, several areas need further exploration. First, the data indicated from the networks theme, the ability to manage several areas was significant, that suggests further research on how to manage multiple networks and the skills required. Second, based on the networks theme, the ability to identify key traits in others is a critical step towards investing in the relationship, this finding indicates further research on how to accurately identify desirable traits in others and provide the proper mentorship to enhance them. Third, the leaders' responses, from the leadership network development theme, showed a leader of leaders (e.g., chief apostle) of multiple networks was essential to create a movement, that suggests further research on what skills are required to lead at that level and how to design a movement. Fourth, from the network influence theme, the ability to shape the network was critical to leaders, which suggest further research on how to evaluate the network, how to shape a network, and what resources are needed. Fifth, the data indicated, from the network leadership influence theme, the ability to achieve goals were necessary, which suggests the need for more research on how to evaluate the status of the network and how to implement change. The findings from the Hayes (2018) study not only provided insights, but additional questions also arose from the study.

Recommendations for Future Practice

The Hayes (2018) study expanded the existing knowledge regarding U.S. leaders' experiences and global networks. All participants mentioned network development from inside the network perspective, suggesting for network leaders the importance of focusing on the environment outside of the network. For example, nonprofit leaders could develop a network focusing inwardly first on building leaders and then outwardly to thrive in the global environment to reach their organizational goals. The act of thriving requires leaders to (a) evaluate the global environment, (b) determine weakness and strengths to exploit in the environment, (c) shape the network to overcome environmental challenges, (d) leverage and implement resources to create environmental opportunities, and (e) forecast the future environment to position the network for success. Therefore, the implications of this research might help both organizations and leaders to develop productive relational networks. The need to investigate how these global relational leaders developed over time through the lens of knowledge, skills, and abilities is an essential implication. In addition, exploring the power of relationships as the tie that strengthens networks at a global level and illustrates the importance of people. The unique power of people and their relationships are often overlooked. Nonprofit leaders who can use a refractive thinking approach in the implementation of effective relational leadership strategies, at the individual and collective levels, might bring long-term success to their organizations.

THOUGHTS FROM THE ACADEMIC ENTREPRENEUR

The problem to be solved:
- Leading and expanding influence through relationships
- Developing and establishing relational leadership and network skill sets

The goals:
- Understanding how to develop global networks to reach organizational goals
- Understanding how to scan the external environment and align the organization for success

The questions to ask:
- How can leaders use relationships to lead effectively?
- How can organizations use relationships to reach goals effectively?

Today's Business Application:
- Effective leaders who understand individual relationships are better equipped to invest in key relationships and develop culture, positioning emerging leaders to leverage culture for success.
- Effective leaders who understand collective relationships are better equipped to shape the network and create opportunities, achieving the organizational goals by exploiting success.
- Effective leaders who understand the external environment are better prepared to align the organization to thrive in the future environment.

REFERENCES

Abosagf, I., Yen, D. A., & Barnes, B. R. (2016). What is dark about the darkside of business relationships? *Industrial Marketing Management, 55,* 5–9. doi:10.1016/j.indmarman.2016.02.008

Anklam, P. (2007). *Net work.* London, UK: Routledge.

Austin, E. W., & Pinkleton, B. E. (2015). *Strategic public relations management: Planning and managing effective communication campaigns.* New York, NY: Routledge.

Balkundi, P., & Kilduff, M. (2006). The ties that lead: A social network approach to leadership. *The Leadership Quarterly, 17,* 419–439. doi:10.1016/j.leaqua.2006.01.001

Brass, D. J., Butterfield, K. D., & Skaggs, B. C. (1998). Relationships and unethical behavior: A social network perspective. *Academy of Management Review, 23*(1), 14–31. doi:10.5465/amr.1998.192955

Burt, R. S. (2004). Structural holes and good ideas. *American Journal of Sociology, 110,* 349–399. doi:10.1086/421787

Burt, R. S. (2009). *Structural holes: The social structure of competition.* Cambridge, MA: Harvard University Press.

Carpenter, M. A., Li, M., & Jiang, H. (2012). Social network research in organizational contexts: A systematic review of methodological issues and choices. *Journal of Management, 38,* 1328–1361. doi:10.1177/0149206312440119

Christerson, B., & Flory, R. (2017). *The rise of network Christianity: How independent leaders are changing the religious landscape.* New York, NY: Oxford University Press.

Cogburn, D. L., & Espinoza-Vasquez, F. K. (2011). From networked nominee to networked nation: Examining the impact of Web 2.0 and social media on political participation and civic engagement in the 2008 Obama campaign. *Journal of Political Marketing, 10*(1-2), 189-213. doi:10.1080/15377857.2011.540224

Cohall, K. G., & Cooper, B. S. (2010). Educating American Baptist pastors: A national survey of church leaders. *Journal of Research on Christian Education, 19*(1), 27–55. doi:10.1080/10656211003630174

Cook, B. (Ed.). (2012). *Aligning with the apostolic: Apostles and the apostolic movement in the seven mountains of culture* (Vol. 1). Lakebay, WA: Kingdom House Publishing.

Cottle, R. (2015). *Apostles are generals and governors.* Retrieved from http://www.icaleaders.com/about-ical/definition-of-apostle/

Cullen, K., & Yammarino, F. J. (2014). Special issue on collective and network approaches to leadership. *The Leadership Quarterly, 25,* 180–181. doi:10.1016/j.leaqua.2013.12.005

Dempwolf, C. S., & Lyles, L. W. (2011). The uses of social network analysis in planning: A review of the literature. *Journal of Planning Literature, 27*(1), 3–21. doi:10.1177/0885412211411092

Dinh, J. E., Lord, R. G., Gardner, W. L., Meuser, J. D., Linden, R. C., & Hu, J. (2014). Leadership theory and research in the new millennium: Current theoretical trends and changing perspectives. *The Leadership Quarterly, 25,* 36–62. doi:10.1016/j.leaqua.2013.11.005

Dutton, J. E., & Ragins, B. R. (2017). *Exploring positive relationships at work: Building a theoretical and research foundation.* New York, NY: Psychology Press.

Emery, C., Calvard, T. S., & Pierce, M. E. (2013). Leadership as an emergent group process: A social network study of personality and leadership. *Group Processes & Intergroup Relations, 16*(1), 28–45. doi:10.1177/1368430212461835

Everton, S. F. (2012). *Disrupting dark networks* (No. 34). New York, NY: Cambridge University Press.

Everton, S. F. (2015). Networks and religion: Ties that bind, loose, build up, and tear down. *Journal of Social Structure, 16*(10), 1–34. Retrieved from https://www.cmu.edu/joss/

Everton, S. F. (2016). Social networks and religious violence. *Review of Religious Research, 58*(2), 191–217. doi:10.1007/s13644-015-0240-3

Fairhurst, G. T., & Connaughton, S. L. (2014). Leadership: A communicative perspective. *Leadership, 10*(1), 7–35. doi:10.1177/1742715013509396

Fang, E., Palmatier, R. W., Scheer, L. K., & Li, N. (2008). Trust at different organizational levels. *Journal of Marketing, 72*(2), 80–98. doi:10.1509/jmkg.72.2.80

Finke, R., & Stark, R. (1988). Religious economies and sacred canopies: Religious mobilization in American cities, 1906. *American Sociological Review, 53*(1), 41–49. doi:10.2307/2095731

Fransen, K., Van Puyenbroeck, S., Loughead, T. M., Vanbeselaere, N., De Cuyper, B., Vande Broek, G., & Boen, F. (2015). Who takes the lead?: Social network analysis as a pioneering tool to investigate shared leadership within sports teams. *Social Networks, 43,* 28–38. doi:10.1016/j.socnet.2015.04.003

Graen, G. B., & Scandura, T. A. (1987). Toward a psychology of dyadic organizing. In L. L. Cummings & B. M. Staw (Eds.), *Research in organizational behavior* (pp. 175–208). Greenwich, CT: JAI Press.

Granovetter, M. S. (1973). The strength of weak ties. *American Journal of Sociology, 78,* 1360–1380. doi:10.1086/225469

Hayes, S. (2018). *Relational leadership and global networks: An exploratory qualitative study* (Doctoral dissertation). Retrieved from Dissertations & Theses, Capella University. (UMI No. 10936492)

Hosking, D. M. (2007). *Not leaders, not followers: A post-modern discourse of leadership processes.* Charlotte, NC: Information Age.

Hosking, D. M., & Bouwen, R. (2000). Organizational learning: Relational-constructionist approaches: An overview. *European Journal of Work and Organizational Psychology, 9*(2), 129–132. doi:10.1080/135943200397897

Iannaccone, L. R. (1994). Why strict churches are strong. *American Journal of Sociology, 99,* 1180–1211. doi:10.1086/230409

Iannaccone, L., Stark, R., & Finke, R. (1998). Rationality and the religious mind. *Economic Inquiry, 36,* 373–389. doi:10.1111/j.1465-7295.1998.tb01721.x

Johnson, T., & Ross, K. (2009). *Atlas of global Christianity, 1910–2010.* Edinburgh, Scotland: Edinburgh University Press.

Kelly, J. (2016). *Apostolic ways for apostolic days.* Retrieved from https://johnpkelly.org/2015/11/25/apostolic-ways-for-apostolic-days/

Kelly, J. (2018a). *Apostolic networks the purpose and value.* Retrieved from https://johnpkelly.org/leadership/#apostolicnetworks/

Kelly, J. (2018b). *Some values and characteristics of an apostolic network.* Retrieved from https://johnpkelly.org/leadership/#apostolicnetworks/

Kerbs, V. E. (2002). Mapping networks of terrorist cells. *Connections, 24*(3), 43–52. Retrieved from http://www.insna.org/connections.html

Kilduff, M., & Krackhardt, D (1994). Bringing the individual back in: A structural analysis of the internal market for reputation in organizations. *Academic Management Journal, 37*(1), 87–108. doi:10.2307/256771

Krackhardt, D., & Hanson, J. R. (1993). Informal networks. *Harvard Business Review, 71,* 104–111. Retrieved from https://hbr.org/

Lindsay, D. M. (2006). Elite power: social networks within American evangelicalism. *Sociology of Religion, 67,* 207-227. doi:10.1093/socrel/67.3.207

Mollick, E. (2014). The dynamics of crowdfunding: An exploratory study. *Journal of Business Venturing, 29*(1), 1-16. doi:10.1016/j.jbusvent.2013.06.005

Moorman, C., Zaltman, G., & Deshpande, R. (1992). Relationships between providers and users of market research: The dynamics of trust within and between organizations. *Journal of Marketing Research, 29,* 314–328. doi:10.2307/3172742

Nyaga, G. N., Lynch, D. F., Marshall, D., & Ambrose, E. (2013). Power asymmetry, adaptation and collaboration in dyadic relationships involving a powerful partner. *Journal of Supply Chain Management, 49*(3), 42–65. doi:10.1111/jscm.12011

Obstfeld, D. (2005). Social networks, the tertius iungens orientation, and involvement in innovation. *Administrative Science Quarterly, 50*, 100–130. doi:10.2189/asqu.2005.50.1.100

O'Reggio, T. (2012). The rise of the new apostolic reformation and its implication for Adventist eschatology. *Journal of the Adventist Theological Society, 23*(2), 131–160. Retrieved from https://digitalcommons.andrews.edu/jats/

Sarros, J. C., Cooper, B. K., & Santora, J. C. (2011). Leadership vision, organizational culture, and support for innovation in not-for-profit and for-profit organizations. *Leadership & Organization Development Journal, 32*, 291-309. doi:10.1108/01437731111123933

Singh, S., Corner, P. D., & Pavlovich, K. (2015). Failed, not finished: A narrative approach to understanding venture failure stigmatization. *Journal of Business Venturing, 30*(1), 150–166. doi:10.1016/j.jbusvent.2014.07.005

Sparrowe, R. T., R. C. Liden, S. J. Wayne, & M. L. Kraimer. (2001). Social networks and the performance of individuals and groups. *Academic Management Journal, 44*, 316–325. doi:10.2307/3069458

Uhl-Bien, M. (2005). Implicit theories of relationships in the workplace. In B. Schyns & J. R. Meindl (Eds.), *Implicit leadership theories: Essays and explorations* (pp. 103–133). Greenwich, CT: Information Age Publishing.

Uhl-Bien, M. (2006). Relational leadership theory: Exploring the social processes of leadership and organizing. *The Leadership Quarterly, 17*, 654–676. doi:10.1016/j.leaqua.2006.10.007

Wang, L., Gopal, R., Shankar, R., & Pancras, J. (2015). On the brink: Predicting business failure with mobile location-based check ins. *Decision Support Systems, 76*, 3–13. doi:10.1016/j.dss.2015.04.010

Wasserman, S., & Faust, K. (1994). *Social network analysis: Methods and applications* (Vol. 8). Cambridge, England: Cambridge University Press.

Weaver, J. (2016). *The new apostolic reformation: History of a modern charismatic movement.* Jefferson, NC: McFarland.

About the Author...

Dr. Samuel L. Hayes, Jr., resides in the historic town of Fayetteville, North Carolina. Dr. Sam holds several accredited degrees: a Bachelor of Science (BS) in Business Management from University of Phoenix; a Master of Business Administration (MBA) from American Intercontinental University, a Master of Science (MS) in Information Strategy and Political Warfare from Naval Postgraduate School; and a Doctorate of Philosophy (PhD) in Organization and Management with a specialization in Leadership from Capella University. He also severed in the U.S. Army as a military intelligence enlisted Solider and as a Cavalry officer. Currently, he is serving in special operations as a Civil Affairs officer, with over a combined 20 years of experience.

Dr. Sam is also the Apostle of His Glory International Ministries and an active member of Kappa Alpha Psi Fraternity, Inc.

He is an impactful author known for a co-authored thesis on *Civil Affairs 2025: The Strategic Design of Civil Affairs,* challenging the status quo to redesign Civil Affairs for the future environment. Additional published works include his dissertation: *Relational Leadership and Global Networks: An Exploratory Qualitative Study, Design Thinking and Civil Affairs' Future, and 82nd Civil Affairs Battalion's Last Deployed Company: Lessons Learned.*

To reach Dr. Samuel Hayes, Jr. for information on networks, strategic design, design thinking, civil affairs community, apostolic networks, guest speaking or consulting, please visit his **website: http://drsamuelhayesjr.com** or **e-mail: drsamuelhayesjr@gmail.com**

CHAPTER 10

Nonprofit Transition Strategies: Combat Boots to Heels

Dr. Julie Ducharme, Dr. Karen Walker & Dr. Cheryl Lentz

The higher education world is a billion-dollar industry with for-profit colleges. These schools, for example, will charge $120,000 dollars for an Associate's Degree program in the culinary arts. Typically, the model of for-profit colleges is that they are run just like a business. This model includes shareholders who expect the college to make money to ensure they make money. Programs that do not meet this profit motive do not exist regardless of the student populations they intend to serve. These challenges of serving the needs of the student, particularly the U.S. military veteran, will be the focus of this chapter using a refractive thinking approach.

What has been called into question recently is the mindset of higher education and particularly the for-profits. According to Silver and Lentz (2012),

> The rise of the adult learning model has removed educational access barriers and enabled more individuals from diverse backgrounds—including women, minorities, full time employees, and students to return to unfinished degrees—to experience intellectual growth and achievement. Subsequently, certain variables have led to a cultural shift from a literature and conceptual focus to one in which students are becoming consumer learners. (p. xi)

The challenge is precisely this shift from students to consumers and clients within these for profit institutions. The refractive thinking approach begs the question whether this has been a positive shift within this paradigm of higher education. "Time is of the essence, as education is now a pursuit of employment, promotion, or transition into a new career rather than merely a journey of intellectual expansion" (Silver & Lentz, 2012, p. 5).

As we watched the closing of Corinthian, Westwood, Sanford, Brown, Marinello Beauty School, and most recently (2016) the giant ITT Technical Institute (ITT TECH), students, families, military veterans, and many more are left to assess whether a for-profit school with such a business money making mindset is the most viable option where they need to attend school. In addition, important programs needed for students lacking in for profits because of this *business* mindset versus a student-centric mindset. The question to ask is should students be looking to nonprofit schools with a different focus on the students and not the money to find their way through their educational goals?

Is the for profit business motive compatible with the needs of the students? "Sociologists Water Powell and Jason Owen-Smith have astutely observed that 'the commercialization of university-based knowledge signals the university's role as a driver of the economy" (Arum & Roksa, 2011, p. 10). The challenge is the shift of the collegiate faculty, no longer simply responsible for the expected course learning objectives. Faculty must also fulfill customer service expectations as well. "Therein lies the quagmire—how do institutions continue to provide integrity programs while meeting market needs for employers and providing viable and intriguing experiences for those who consume the material?" (Silver & Lentz, 2012, p. 6). Ultimately, the question to ask is whether the business of higher education is getting in the way of the focus of educating students.

According to Ruch (2001),

> Many who have crossed over (to the for profit side) find that there is a certain refreshing honesty associated with being openly for profit, a welcoming lack of pretense in the economic exchange between students and their institutions ... particularly not having to deal with the tenure system. (p. 21)

The advantages include, according to Ruch, the ability of administrative freedom of quick decision-making in response to market demands created in less than a year. Additional control of both topic and what is taught in the classroom by faculty is hailed as a victory in this cross over, no longer constrained by the traditional glacial pace of change in traditional academic, not driven by business performance demands and response to market needs.

> There was a time when going to college was regarded as a privilege. Prior to 1980s, students were expected to exhibit gratitude and humility for the opportunity to study with professors and many of them did. Today, however going to college is viewed by many as a right and a consumable good. (Ruch, 2001, p. 79)

Nonprofit universities are typically more affordable and have more degree options than their counterpart for-profit schools (Oherrin, 2011). Typically, the focus is more on the *student* than profit. Nonprofit institutions of higher learning want the student to reach those academic goals. Nonprofits work hard to serve the **students,** instead of the **shareholders.** Nonprofits often have additional funding coming in from other sources to include: donors, grants, and endowments; For-profit schools will raise tuition cost often to keep the business afloat because they do not have the nonprofit financial support (Oherrin, 2011).

According to Washburn (2005), the movement toward privatization of higher education grew from the need in the 1970s to compete with Japan and other countries,

A powerful nexus of political, economic, and industrial forces began pushing America's universities to forge closer ties with private industry, convert themselves into engines of economic growth and pump out commercially valuable new inventions. More and more the job of teaching students was shunted to the side, even though the universities' most important public function was to nurture intellectual creativity and talent. The reformers who pushed these changes were, for the most part, motivated by noble intentions, genuinely believing that universities' could take on these functions without compromising their core educational mission. (p. xi)

The true challenge was not in these relationships with industry—as these have been in place since the time of apprenticeship and vocational programs; the challenge was in the "elimination of any clear boundary in separating academia from commerce" (Washburn, 2005, p. xi). Thus, the question remains, are the lines between the profit motive and the needs of the students mutually exclusive?

As the issues with for-profit schools continue, more and more nonprofit educational, centers, technical / vocational colleges, universities, and more have not surfaced with a student-centered / academic focus. In this emerging digital age, new innovative educational delivery models emerged, including those who recognized a vast population of nontraditional learners declassified with existing educational delivery models. The traditional model of holding classes during the daytime through a predominant lecture modality are no longer the status quo, obsolescing this antiquated educational model (Silver & Lents, 2012). In particular, there is a new student popular flooding all schools, for-profit, nonprofit, and educational institutions trying to learn how to best serve this new population within these emerging innovative models. In particular are the needs of the U.S. military veteran. "The American Council on Education (ACE predication almost 2 million veterans returning from the Iraq and Afghanistan Wars were expected on the college campuses across the country" (Kelley, Smith, & Fox, 2013, p. 3). Additionally, "over two million servicemember's serving since 2001 are expected to receive the higher education incentives offered from the GI Bill" (Oherrin, 2011, p. 3). Because of this increase, colleges and universities observed a substantial increase in veteran enrollment. An even more staggering statistic is that 30%-40% of military veterans will leave the post-secondary education prior to completing their degree because of difficulty in transitioning back to civilian life and as well civilian work (McCasline, 2013). Higher education for-profit institutions continue to struggle to create successful veteran transition programs for students (McCaslin, 2013).

This new group of student veterans, active duty, separated, and retired, brings a unique problem for traditional and for-profit higher educational programs. What colleges and universities fail to recognize is that the veterans are, by definition, nontraditional students. Veterans are not in the typical 18-21 range, but older and often a transfer student because of many college credits they earned while serving in the military. These additional stats on military veterans may help shed light on the uniqueness of this emerging student population and how serving them requires programs uniquely focused on veterans' needs as compared to a traditional student.

- "Forty-three percent of students with military experience attended public two-year institutions, 21% attended public four-year institutions, 12% enrolled in private non-profit institutions, and 12% enrolled in private for-profit institutions" (Kelley et al., 2013, p. 3).
- "Veterans tend to be older and are more likely to be non-white than traditional college students" (Kelley et al., 2013, p. 4).
- "Women currently makeup nearly 15% of the military and are a rapidly growing segment of the veteran population (Business and Professional Women Foundation, 2007); 27% of students with military experience are women" (Kelley et al., 2013, p. 4).

Recent efforts show options for existing programs at educational institutions of higher education for veterans in a national survey by the American Council on Education (Cook & Kim, 2009) with other higher education organizations. In this survey, more than 700 hundred universities and colleges participated in explaining their veteran-specific program or service (or lack thereof) (Cook & Kim, 2009).

According to this survey, over half of the institutions responded, as 57% do provide some sort of program or services for veterans, but not one has a specific *transition program* that they have provided (Cook & Kim, 2009). Sixty percent of these institutions that responded said that creating programs for the military were part of their long-term plans (American Counsel Survey, 2015, as cited in Cook & Kim 2009). These lack of program options are a cause for a large number of higher educational institutions facing unique challenges when attempting to serve a veteran student population (Jones, 2013). Consequently, a gap exists regarding the specific challenges of military student veterans and their transition back to civilian life and the civilian workforce. The gap is that not enough transition programs specifically target veterans. No evidence from our study so far indicates any programs that specifically support women veterans in particular in their transition the way our *Combat Boots to Heels* program does.

Combat Boots to Heels Program

Our unique transition program serves a need to provide a professional development program for female veterans that begins with an assessment of competencies proven necessary for success as leaders. This program helps to assess where they are to build a plan tailored for where the individual wants to go.

When the veteran leaves the military, they could have 4 years or 24 years of service in one job field or in many job fields. They were often the experts in their fields and are seen as mentors by many in their military professions. When they leave the military, the service member often struggles to find their identity again in the civilian world (Culbreth, Newsome, & Whiting, 2013).

The faster we can assist veterans by closing this identity gap the better. Our program, *Combat Boots to Heels*, jumps right on this with our F-SET Inventory assessment at enrollment. Our assessment helps as a bridge to enable the veteran to do self-assessment with one of our trained expert consultants in a guided interview process. We are able to work with the veteran over five modules that assess the key components of our program: femininity, self-efficacy, emotional intelligence (EI), and teamwork. The fifth module provides a framework to ensure they have resources for follow on employment if needed and to further showcase the veteran in their new venue and professional arenas with our alumni network.

The F-SET Inventory is based on the F-SET model of leadership proven for effectiveness (Walker, 2012). Each element of the F-SET Inventory has additional facets that are measured; however, the four main components are: femininity, self-efficacy, EI, and teamwork. We provided further breakdowns of each component with evidences tied in the military settings.

Femininity

Previous leadership research focused on gender stereotyping and social role theory. For instance, Eagly and Karau's (2002) social-role theory included discussion of two kinds of expectations for leaders: agentic and communal. Agentic characteristics are more strongly ascribed to men, described as primarily assertive, controlling, and confident tendency—"aggressive, ambitious, dominant, forceful, independent, self-sufficient, self-confident, and prone to act as a leader" (Eagly & Karau, 2002, p. 580). Communal characteristics are more strongly ascribed to women, related to a concern for the welfare of other people—for example, "affectionate, helpful, kind, sympathetic, interpersonally sensitive, nurturing, and gentle" (Eagly & Karau, 2002, p. 580). Communal and agentic qualities are required for successful leadership in business or the military sector.

The true objective of this argument is in negating the traditional perception that agentic leadership is more successful than communal leadership, especially in a military setting that is often assumed to endorse authoritarian leaders (Walker, 2008). Leadership research concerning women military officers specifically contradicts previous social-role research. According to Walker (2008), women officers have an advantage as leaders in the military leading in a male dominated environment. The scarcity of women in top level positions warrants a unique leadership approach that calls for aspects of femininity, self-efficacy, emotional intelligence, and teamwork.

Self-efficacy

Contradictory to the general perception that more agentic qualities are ascribed to leaders, women officers in the U.S. Navy and U.S. Marine Corps (Walker, 2012) argued that maintaining their femininity is a key part of endorsing high self-efficacy, confidence. and competence as a leader. There is no longer a need for female officers to *act like a man* to be considered a successful leader. The main premise behind this argument is that the ability to be oneself and not feel obligated to endorse agentic qualities as leaders positively affects self-efficacy. When a leader is confident in their abilities and who they are, this confidence directly relates to their overall feeling of competency and self-efficacy.

Self efficacy is defined as an individual's belief about their capabilities to produce designated levels of performance (Judge, Jackson, Shaw, Scott, & Rich, 2007). This concept significantly applies to organizational research, which utilized self-efficacy as a related variable in training, leadership, newcomer socialization and adjustment, performance evaluation, stress, negotiation, and work-related performance (Judge et al., 2007). A leader's expectations about goal accomplishment will affect the performance of his or her followers. For example, the Pygmalion effect occurs when leaders express high expectations for followers, which results in high performance from followers (Judge et al., 2007). Conversely, the Golem effect refers to leaders expressing low expectations for followers, which results in low or non-existent performance from followers. A leader must first be confident in personal expectations to better understand how best to influence or impact the organization in which they lead.

Emotional Intelligence

In addition to self-efficacy, leadership includes the importance of emotional intelligence. EI is the ability to understand and express emotion in thought, reason with emotion, and regulate emotions within oneself or others (Roberts, Zeidner, & Matthews, 2001). Current conceptualization of EI focuses on one's "ability to accurately identify, appraise, and discriminate among emotions in oneself and others, understand emotions, assimilate emotions in thought and regulate both positive and negative emotions in self and others" (Roberts et al., 2001, p. 198). This trait can be extremely influential in leadership. The question is: do women officers have an upper hand in this aspect?

EI is a controversial topic with broad ranges of results inconsistent with a purely situational explanation of gender differences; however results are consistent with the notion that men and women are socialized to express emotion and empathy in different ways. These differences are incumbent upon the individual's perception and how they believe they should regulate emotion and thought. Women in the workplace display more sensitivity to problems associated with interpersonal relations than men do (Porter & Stone 1995). Researchers also reported that women seek social support, using emotion-focused coping with their mood to a greater extent than men, whereas men use more problem-focused coping than women (Butler & Nolen-Hoeksema, 1994). As leaders, women may indeed have the upper hand when it comes to human relations and more insight into dealing with emotional occurrences in the workplace. Because of the scarcity of women in the military, as a woman military officer EI then becomes a unique gift for reading people and their emotions to develop more effective leader / follower relationships.

Teamwork

The leader / follower relationship is based on trust and focuses on the social exchange created between the leader and member. Behavior in the workplace may then be positively or negatively affected by implications of this relationship. The Center for Creative Leadership found that the number one variable for success in the top three jobs in large organizations was *relationships with subordinates*. (Kouzes & Posner, 2002). The key here is the acknowledgement of how *one* affects the whole.

An individual's impact on an organization is further endorsed by the transformational leadership concept. The transformational leader expresses a collective vision and inspires followers to look past self-interests for the good of the organization. Historically, the transformational leader has been attributed with more communal characteristics as opposed to the agentic characteristics of traditional leadership principles. Anderson, Lievens, Dam, and Born's (2006) findings supported this concept among female British Army officer candidates rated higher on constructs reflecting an interpersonally oriented leadership style, specifically oral communication and interaction. Female candidates were also evaluated to have higher levels of drive and determination (Anderson et al., 2006).

Berdahl and Anderson (2005) further examined women's transformational and decentralized approach to leadership. Their study addressed sex differences in centralized (one or a few group members) and decentralized (shared among members) structures of group leadership (Berdahl & Anderson, 2005). A centralized structure generally leads to lower levels of cohesion, satisfaction, and performance; and to higher levels of tardiness, absenteeism, and turnover. The decentralized structure in contrast, allows more cohesion and a joint effort at leadership tasks. The results of their longitudinal study were that groups with fewer men in them have less centralized leadership structures; and group work was perceived more positively with a decentralized leadership style and equality in groups (Berdahl & Anderson, 2005).

The teamwork concept produces a **we** not **me** consensus in the organization and aids in mission accomplishment for the individual and the whole. Women officer's transformational leadership style is more likely to focus on team-oriented goals within the organization.

Reaping the Rewards of *Combat Boots to Heels*

The alumni of Combat Boots to Heels showcase their talents through a valuable network of alumni. They complete five modules and a comprehensive assessment with a tailored expert coach, able to match their competency with their passion to regain the confidence they need to either jump into a new career field or excel / exceed their goals in an existing field.

One example is an alumnus who was in the administrative profession for over 8 years in the U.S. Marine Corps and U.S. Army National Guard combined. Her true passion was in creative art design, however, she struggled to find the confidence to jump into a new career. We surveyed her competencies with the F-SET Inventory and then explored her passion with teaching art. She was well on her way to starting her own business by the end of the course. Her revenue was $60k in the first 2 months after launching her own Etsy website to sell her art products and she opened her own studio to teach art.

There are several others that have similar endings. The program has been active since Fall 2017 and we have been fortunate enough to have eight enrolled. We work with voluntary enrollment because this is a professional development program and involves ample amounts of self-reflection, dedication, and commitment to the process of professional development. Our completion rate is 80%. Some veterans do get pulled back into other commitments for Reserve Military duty or more demanding career fields (realty, contracting, etc.). We use an innovative approach through the non-profit vocational college and the F-SET Inventory to make *Combat Boots to Heels* a success story for the individual female veteran.

Conclusion

This emerging model of higher education that includes shareholders who expect the college to make money to ensure they make money may be a challenge regarding the effectiveness of institutions of higher learning. These challenges of serving the needs of the student, particularly the U.S. military veteran call into question the mindset of higher education, particularly the for-profits. The refractive thinking approach to this chapter offered analysis of the needs of serving nontraditional students, particularly asking the question regarding the boundary of academia and commerce. The question pursued in this chapter was whether these emerging business models serve the needs of nontraditional students in particular and U.S. veterans specifically.

THOUGHTS FROM THE ACADEMIC ENTREPRENEUR

The problem to be solved:
- Women in the Military are not transitioning confidently into civilian life and jobs

The goals:
- Understanding how implementing a successful transition program in a nonprofit setting will lead women in the military to better transition to life and work

The questions to ask:
- How can military women successfully transition back to civilian life and work with confidence?
- What leadership characteristics can military women use to transition into business life successfully?

Today's Business Application:
- Non-profit vocational colleges can offer transferable skills for veterans.
- Veterans are an increasing population group that is highly talented entering higher education, then looking for careers.
- Non-profit higher education institutions can better serve the needs of the students because they can provide professional development, mentoring, and alumni networking without additional charges to the student as a financial burden.
- The nonprofit gains in popularity and purpose as it continues to serve the need of the student.

REFERENCES

Anderson, N., Lievens, F., van Dam, K., & Born, M. (2006). A construct-driven investigation of gender differences in a leadership-role assessment center. *Journal of Applied Psychology, 91*, 555-566. https://dx.doi.org/10.1037/0021-9010.91.3.555

Arum, R., & Roksa, J. (2011). *Academically adrift: Limited learning on college campuses.* Chicago, IL University of Chicago Press.

Berdahl, J., & Anderson, C. (2005). Men, women, and leadership centralization in groups over time. *Group Dynamics: Theory, Research, and Practice, 9*(1), 45-57. https://dx.doi.org/10.1037/1089-2699.9.1.45

Butler, L., & Nolen-Hoeksema, S. (1994). Gender differences in responses to depressed mood in a college sample. *Sex Roles, 30*(5-6), 331-346. Retrieved from https://link.springer.com/article/10.1007/BF01420597

Cook, B. J., & Kim, Y. (2009). *From soldier to student: easing the transition of service members on Campus.* Washington, DC: American Association of State Colleges and Universities.

Culbreth, M., Newsome, G. & Whiting, P. (2013). Bridging the gap between veterans and civilian clinicians. Retrieved from https://www.counseling.org/docs/default-source/vistas/article_7839cd23f16116603abcacff0000bee5e7.pdf?sfvrsn=6

Department of Defense (DOD). (2002). Women in defense. *Defense Link, 11*(31). Retrieved from http://www.defenselink.mil/prhome/poprep2002/appendixb/b_32.htm

Eagly, A., & Karau, S. (2002). Role congruity theory of prejudice toward female leaders. *Psychological Review, 109*, 573-598. https://dx.doi.org/10.1037//0033-295x.109.3.573

Jones, K. (2013). Understanding student veterans in transition. *The Qualitative Report, 18*(74), 1-14.

Judge, T., Jackson, C., Shaw, J., Scott, B., & Rich, B. (2007). Self-efficacy and work-related performance: The integral role of individual differences. *Journal of Applied Psychology, 92*(1), 107-127. https://dx.doi.org/10.1037/0021-9010.92.1.107

Kelley, B., Smith, J., & Fox, E. (2013). *Preparing your campus for veterans' success: An integrated approach to facilitating the transition and persistence of our military students.* Sterling, VA: Stylus Publishing, LLC.

Kouzes, J., & Posner, B. (2002). *The leadership challenge.* San Francisco, CA: Josey-Bass A Wiley Company.

McCaslin, S. E., Leach, B., Herbst, E., M., & Armstrong, K., (2013). Overcoming barriers to care for returning veterans: Expanding services to college campuses. *Journal of Rehabilitation Research and Development, 50*(8), vii-xiv. https://dx.doi.org/10.1682/jrrd.2013.09.0204

O'Herrin, E. (2011). Enhancing veteran success in higher education. *Peer Review, 13*(1), 15-18.

Porter, L., & Stone, A. (1995). Are there really gender differences in coping? A reconsideration of previous data and results from a daily study. *Journal of Social and Clinical Psychology, 14*(2), 184-202. https://dx.doi.org/10.1521/jscp.1995.14.2.184

Roberts, R., Zeidner, M., & Matthews, G. (2001). Does emotional intelligence meet traditional standards for an intelligence? Some new data and conclusions. *Emotion, 1*(3), 196-231. https://dx.doi.org/10.1037//1528-3542.1.3.196

Ruch, R. (2001). *Higher Ed, Inc.: The rise of the for-profit university*. Baltimore, MD: The Johns Hopkins University Press.

Silver, G., & Lentz, C. (2012). *The consumer learner: Emerging expectations of a customer service mentality in post-secondary education*. Las Vegas, NV: Pensiero Press.

Uniformed Services Almanac Inc. (2007). *Uniformed services almanac*. Falls Church, VA: Uniformed Services Almanac.

Walker, K. M. (2008). *Women leading men: A look into the phenomenon of leadership from the perspective of women officers in the military*. Retrieved from ProQuest Dissertations and Theses database. (UMI No. 3324)

Walker, K. M. (2012). A model for femininity and military leadership. *Journal of Psychological Issues in Organizational Culture, 2*(4), 22-37. https://dx.doi.org/10.1002/jpoc.20086

Washburn, J. (2005). *University Inc.: The corporate corruption of higher education*. Cambridge, MA: Basic Books as part of Perseus Publishing.

Women's Memorial. (2003). *Women in military service for America memorial*. Retrieved from https://www.womensmemorial.org/

About the Authors...

For the last 15 years, Dr. Julie Ducharme has been working with corporations, colleges, and universities in San Diego and outside of San Diego as well. Dr. Julie holds a BA in communication, a MBA with a specialization in marketing, and a DBA with a specialization in Leadership. Dr. Julie is a public speaker and has spoken with and at many universities across the United States and corporations on leadership, business, and marketing.

Dr. Julie is also a published author with a children's book, *Amy the Clumsy Angel*, a master thesis published and her most recent publication her dissertation on *Women in Senior Leadership Positions in Academia*, and *Leading By My Ponytail: Why Can't I Wear Pink and Be President?*

She currently is the owner / creator / CEO of JD Consulting LLC, and the owner / creator / CEO of *Julie's Party People*. She regularly consults with businesses and schools in various areas of business, public outreach, curriculum, program design, and many other topics in the business realm to include veterans' transition programs such as *Combat Boots to Heels*.

To reach Dr. Julie, please **email: juliemducharme@gmail.com**

Dr. Karen Walker is an advocate for change and a subject matter expert in leadership, gender issues, and workplace psychometrics. She is a published author (**www.leadingbymyponytail.com**), has been involved in various public speaking engagements, co-hosts the Empowering Your Pink Podcast (**http://empoweringyourpink.libsyn.com/**) and has competed for over 10 years in All-Marine basketball across the Nation. As a Marine Reserve Officer, she has been dedicated to diversity and inclusion events including engagement recruiting activities for female and minority officers. Her Federal service has spanned the Department of the Navy, Department of Homeland Security, the U.S. Secret Service, Department of Transportation, and the Federal Aviation Administration. In 2018, Dr. Karen launched her own business, KW Productions, an expansive organization offering a library of innovative tools that *predict the future*. The tools are proprietary to KW Productions, although certification and licensure for consultants who work in management consulting and similar fields are offered. KW Productions offers assessments in the area of: leadership development, organizational behaviors, climate assessments, personality measurement, and much more. **www.kw-productions.com**

Dr. Karen also gives her time to many non-profit organizations that engage and enrich veteran women or the youth communities. In 2017, she started a professional development program for women veterans called *Combat Boots to Heels* through the Synergy Learning Institute, a nonprofit vocational college. The program helps women veterans in any stage of their transition from the military measuring where they are and helping them build a confident path towards where they want to be. **http://www.synergylearninginstitute.org/combat-boots-to-heels/**

To reach Dr. Karen M. Walker, LtCol, USMCR, please **email: DrCombatPink@gmail.com**

Dr. Cheryl A. Lentz affectionately known as *Doc C* to her students, is a university professor on faculty with Embry-Riddle University, Grand Canyon University (GCU), University of Phoenix, and Walden University. Dr. Cheryl serves as a dissertation mentor / chair and committee member. She is also a dissertation coach, offering expertise as a professional editor for APA style for graduate thesis and doctoral dissertations, as well as journal publications and books.

Dr. Cheryl holds a BA in Music History from the University of Illinois, Champaign-Urbana, a MSIR with a specialization in International Relations, and a Doctorate of Management in Organizational Leadership. Dr. Cheryl is a public speaker at many universities across the United States and in Europe, as well as consults with corporations on leadership, marketing, and publishing.

Awards include: Walden Faculty of the Year, DBA Program, 2016, UOP community service award, and 18 writing awards.

Dr. Cheryl is also an active member of Alpha Sigma Alpha Sorority.

She is an international best-selling author with more than 38 publications known for her writings on *The Golden Palace Theory of Management* and refractive thinking. Additional published works include her dissertation: *Strategic Decision Making in Organizational Performance, Journey Outside the Golden Palace, The Consumer Learner, Technology That Tutors, Effective Study Skills, The Dissertation Toolbox,* International Best Seller: *The Expert Success Solution,* and contributions to the award-winning series: *The Refractive Thinker®: Anthology of Doctoral Learners, Volumes I-XV.*

To reach Dr. Cheryl Lentz for information on refractive thinking, professional editing, radio show guest, or public speaking, please visit her **websites: http://www.DrCherylLentz.com http://www.LentzLeadership.com** or **e-mail: drcheryllentz@gmail.com**

Index

A
Adaptability, 133, 135, 138, 140, 142
African American Women Administrators, 88, 92
Agility, 133, 135, 136, 138, 140
Alternative to incarceration, 148, 154, 156
American Council on Education, 90, 188, 192
Apostolic networks, 169, 170

B
Blogging, 2, 3, 8, 12, 13

C
Coaching, 136–142
Cognitive behavioral programs, 157
Collaboration, 33, 35, 91, 117, 151
Combat Boots to Heels, 187, 192, 193, 197, 198
Community college(s), 87–94, 96–98
Consumer learner, 189
Coping strategies, 91, 93, 97
Corporate financial distress, 47
Corporate governance practices, 46, 47
Criminal justice system, 147–150, 156, 157
Cryptography, 73, 77
Cyber breach, 69, 70, 72

D
Depression, 114
Dimensions of financial distress, 51
Donations, 1–13

E
Emotional intelligence, 193–195

F
Facebook, 2–5, 8–10, 12, 13
Families, 4, 9, 113, 119, 148, 151–157, 188
Feedback, 8, 74, 111, 136, 138–142
Femininity, 193–194
Flexibility, 132, 133, 135, 138, 140, 142
For-profit colleges, 187,
F-SET Inventory assessment, 193

G
Gendered based programs, 156
Global networks, 163, 173, 176–178
Global social networks, 165, 166, 173, 175

H
Higher education administration, 88, 92, 97

I
Imperfect technologies, 71,73, 78
Inmates, 147, 149–151, 157
Instagram, 3, 9, 10, 12, 13
Institutional practices,91, 96, 98

K
Knowledge as a valuable resource, 21, 37
Knowledge change, 21–24, 27, 31, 34–36

Knowledge economy, 26, 27, 35

M
Marketing manager, 2–5, 7–11, 13
Marketing strategies, 1
Mass incarceration, 147, 148, 153
Mental illness, 154, 155, 158
Mentoring, 57, 92, 93, 97, 112, 136, 137, 139–142
Mid-level manager, 90, 134
Military experience, 191

N
Nonprofit leaders, 163–165, 171, 176–179
NPO success, 25

O
Organizational leader, 1, 36, 37, 70, 105, 132, 134, 135, 140, 172

P
Pinterest, 2, 3, 7, 12, 13
Prison reform, 156
Profit margin, 46

R
Recidivism, 147, 148, 153, 155, 156
Relational Leadership Theory, 165, 166
Relational leadership, 163, 165, 166, 167, 173, 175, 177, 179
Remote health monitoring, 75
Risk factors contributing to financial distress, 49, 50

S
Selection practices, 87, 93, 97, 98
Self-awareness, 132, 136, 138, 141, 142

Self-efficacy, 136, 193–195
Senior noncommissioned officers, 136
Sensitive personal information, 69, 71
Social media strategies, 2, 10, 13
Social media, 1–3, 5–11, 77
Social network analysis, 165, 168
Societal barriers, 90,
Substance abuse, 114, 151, 154, 155

T
Task performance, 22, 32
Teamwork, 120, 193, 194, 196, 197
Technological ease, 26, 32
Technological upset, 28, 30, 33,
Texas Community Colleges, 87, 88, 92, 93, 98
Therapy, 155,
Top-level manager, 134,
Twitter, 2, 3, 5, 6, 8–12, 13

U
U.S. military veteran, 187, 188, 198
Understanding employee turnover, 106,
Unlearning, 21–38

V
Veteran transition, 191,
Veterans, 188, 189, 191–193, 198

W
War on drugs, 147, 153,
Women veterans, 192

Y
YouTube, 2, 10–13

The Refractive Thinker®

2019 CATALOG

The Refractive Thinker®: An Anthology of Higher Learning

The Refractive Thinker® Press

info@refractivethinker.com
www.RefractiveThinker.com
blog: www.DissertationPublishing.com

Individual authors own the copyright to their individual materials. The Refractive Thinker® Press has each author's permission to reprint.

Books are available through The Refractive Thinker® Press at special discounts for bulk purchases for the purpose of sales promotion, seminar attendance, or educational purposes. Special volumes can be created for specific purposes and to organizational specifications. Orders placed on www.RefractiveThinker.com for students and military receive a 15% discount. Please contact us for further details.

Refractive Thinker® logo by Joey Root; The Refractive Thinker® Press logo design by Jacqueline Teng, cover design by Peri Poloni-Gabriel, Knockout Design (knockoutbooks.com), cover design & production by Gary A. Rosenberg (thebookcouple.com).

> I *think* therefore I am.
> —Renee Descartes

I *critically think* to be.
I *refractively think* to change the world.

THANK YOU FOR JOINING US as we continue to celebrate the accomplishments of doctoral scholars affiliated with many phenomenal institutions of higher learning. The purpose of the anthology series is to share a glimpse into the scholarly works of participating authors on various subjects.

The Refractive Thinker® serves the tenets of leadership, which is not simply a concept outside of the self, but comes from within, defining our very essence; where the search to define leadership becomes our personal journey, not yet a finite destination.

The Refractive Thinker® is an intimate expression of who we are: the ability to think beyond the traditional boundaries of thinking and critical thinking. Instead of mere reflection and evaluation, one challenges the very boundaries of the constructs itself. If thinking is *inside* the box, and critical thinking is *outside* the box, we add the next step of refractive thinking, *beyond* the box. Perhaps the need exists to dissolve the box completely. The authors within these pages are on a mission to change the world. They are never satisfied or quite content with *what is* or asking *why*, instead these authors intentionally strive to push and test the limits to ask *why not*.

We look forward to your interest in discussing future opportunities. Let our collection of authors continue the journey initiated with Volume I, to which *The Refractive Thinker*® will serve as our guide to future volumes. Come join us in our quest to be refractive thinkers and add your wisdom to the collective. We look forward to your stories.

Please contact The Refractive Thinker® Press for information regarding these authors and the works contained within these pages. Perhaps you or your organization may be looking for an author's expertise to incorporate as part of your annual corporate meetings as a keynote or guest speaker(s), perhaps to offer individual, or group seminars or coaching, or require their expertise as consultants.

Join us on our continuing adventures of *The Refractive Thinker*® where we expand the discussion specifically begun in Volume I: Leadership; Volume II (Editions 1–3): Research Methodology; Volume III: Change Management; Volume IV: Ethics, Leadership, and Globalization; Volume V: Strategy in Innovation; Volume VI: Post-Secondary Education; Volume VII: Social Responsibility; Volume VIII: Effective Business Practices in Motivation & Communication; Volume IX: Effective Business Practices in Leadership & Emerging Technologies; Volume X: Effective Business Strategies for the Defense Industry Sector; Volume XI: Women in Leadership; Volume XII: Cybersecurity in an Increasingly Insecure World; and Volume XIV: Healthcare: The Impact on Leadership, Business, and Education. All our volumes are themed to explore the realm of strategic thought, creativity, and innovation.

Dr. Cheryl A. Lentz, managing editor of The Lentz Leadership Institute, explains the unique benefits of the books for readers:

"They celebrate the diffusion of innovative refractive thinking through the writings of these doctoral scholars as they dare to think differently in search of new applications and understandings of research. Unlike most academic books that merely define research, The Refractive Thinker® *offers unique applications of research from the perspective of multiple authors—each offering a chapter based on their specific expertise."*

THE REFRACTIVE THINKER® PRESS

Volume I: An Anthology of Higher Learning

Volume II, 1st through 3rd Editions: Research Methodology

Volume III: Change Management

Volume IV: Ethics, Leadership, and Globalization

Volume V: Strategy in Innovation

Volume VI: Post-Secondary Education

Volume VII: Social Responsibility

Volume VIII: Effective Business Practices for Motivation and Communication

Volume IX: Effective Business Practices in Leadership & Emerging Technologies

Volume X: Effective Business Strategies for the Defense Industry Sector

Volume XI: Women in Leadership

Volume XII: Cybersecurity in an Increasingly Insecure World

Volume XIII: Entrepreneurship: Growing the Future of Business

Volume XIV: Healthcare: The Impact on Leadership, Business, and Education

Volume XV: Nonprofits: Strategies for Effective Management

Refractive Thinker volumes are available in e-book, Kindle®, iPad®, Nook®, and Sony Reader™, as well as individual e-chapters by author.

COMING SOON FROM THE REFRACTIVE THINKER®!
AVAILABLE THRU THE LENTZ LEADERSHIP INSTITUTE
The Refractive Thinker®: Volume XVI: Generations

Telephone orders: Call us at 702.719.9214

Email Orders: drcheryllentz@gmail.com

Website orders: Please place orders through our website: www.RefractiveThinker.com

COMING IN 2019

The Refractive Thinker® Volume XVI: Generations: Strategies for Managing Generations in the Workforce

Join contributing scholars as they discuss research on effective management of multiple generations in the work force, from Gen Z to Baby Boomers. The focus is on each of the generation's unique and diverse aspects pertaining to employment and management. This volume will continue to shape the conversation of their future success and examine proven strategies for continued excellence.

The Refractive Thinker® Volume XV: Nonprofits: Strategies for Effective Management

In this key volume, contributing scholars discuss research focused on nonprofit organizations and their specific needs regarding strategies for effective management. This volume continues to shape the conversation of their future success and the latest best practices and proven strategies for success.

For more information, please visit our website: www.RefractiveThinker.com

#1 AMAZON BEST SELLER

The Refractive Thinker®: Volume XIV: Healthcare: The Impact on Leadership, Business, and Education

Dr. Gladys Taylor McGarey is internationally known for her pioneer work in alternative medicine. She says it is not about killing off a disease, but seeing the patient as a whole person. She believes that the practice of medicine has become a war against disease—rather than building life, we are destroying it. As we support the living process in a person, life itself brings about the healing that the person needs. Our job as physicians is to work and support the "Physician Within" each of us. Then, living medicine becomes our dwelling place.

The Refractive Thinker®: Volume XIII: Entrepreneurship: Growing the Future of Business

Join Clarissa Burt and contributing scholars as they discuss current research regarding the future of business and the influence of the entrepreneur. This volume contains research shaping the conversation on what the future may hold to success of the economy in the hands of the emerging and evolving small business owner and entrepreneur. As you read, ask yourself: "What should I be doing as an entrepreneur to contribute to the world economy as well as my own success?" Be a refractive thinker as part of the solution to reap the benefits promised in this new digital age.

For more information, please visit our website: www.RefractiveThinker.com

The Refractive Thinker®: Volume XII: Cybersecurity in an Increasingly Insecure World

Join contributing scholars as they discuss current research regarding the challenges of the world of cybersecurity and its effects in and on the marketplace. This volume contains research shaping the conversation regarding what the future may hold to protect businesses and consumers regarding the perils of digital technology.

The Refractive Thinker®: Volume XI: Women in Leadership

Sally Helgesen and contributing scholars discuss research that will influence how women's leadership is understood and supported in the years ahead. They also offer fresh insights into mentoring and coaching practices, the impact of continued shifts in demographics, and the role of women in specific cultures in articulating a sustainable vision of the future. Such contributions will expand and enrich the programmatic offerings that help speed women on their leadership journeys into the future.

For more information, please visit our website: www.RefractiveThinker.com

PUBLICATIONS ORDER FORM

Please send the following books from The Refractive Thinker®:
- ❏ Volume I: An Anthology of Higher Learning
- ❏ Volume II: Research Methodology
- ❏ Volume II: Research Methodology, 2nd Edition
- ❏ Volume II: Research Methodology, 3rd Edition
- ❏ Volume III: Change Management
- ❏ Volume IV: Ethics, Leadership, and Globalization
- ❏ Volume V: Strategy in Innovation
- ❏ Volume VI: Post-Secondary Education
- ❏ Volume VII: Social Responsibility
- ❏ Volume VIII: Effective Business Practices
- ❏ Volume IX: Effective Business Practices in Leadership & Emerging Technologies
- ❏ Volume X: Effective Business Strategies for the Defense Industry Sector
- ❏ Volume XI: Women in Leadership
- ❏ Volume XII: Cybersecurity
- ❏ Volume XIII: Entrepreneurship
- ❏ Volume XIV: Healthcare
- ❏ Volume XV: Nonprofits

Please contact the Refractive Thinker® Press for book prices, e-book prices, and shipping. Individual e-chapters available by author: $3.95 (plus applicable tax).   www.RefractiveThinker.com

- ❏ So You Think You Can Edit?
- ❏ The Expert Success Solution
- ❏ The Unbounded Dimensions Series
- ❏ Ethics, Employment Law, and Faith-Based Universities
- ❏ Effective Study Skills in 5 Simple Steps
- ❏ Technology That Tutors
- ❏ Siberian Husky Rescue
- ❏ The Consumer Learner
- ❏ Journey Outside the Golden Palace
- ❏ The Dissertation Toolbox

Please send more FREE information:
❏ Speaking engagements   ❏ Educational seminars   ❏ Consulting

Join our mailing list:

Name: _____

Address: _____

City: _____ State: _____ Zip: _____

Telephone: _____ Email: _____

E-mail form to: **The Refractive Thinker® Press:** drcheryllentz@gmail.com

Participation in Future Volumes of
The Refractive Thinker®

Yes, I would like to participate in:

❏ **Doctoral Volume**(s) for a specific university or organization:

Name: _____

Contact Person: _____

Telephone: _____ E-mail: _____

❏ **Specialized Volume**(s) Business or Themed:

Name: _____

Contact Person: _____

Telephone: _____ E-mail: _____

E-mail form to: The Refractive Thinker® Press
drcheryllentz@gmail.com
www.RefractiveThinker.com

• Join us on Twitter, LinkedIn, and Facebook

www.ingramcontent.com/pod-product-compliance
Lightning Source LLC
Chambersburg PA
CBHW052022070526
44584CB00016B/1861